D1083843

THE TRIAL OF
ANDREW JOHNSON

Also by Noel B. Gerson

Edict of Nantes
Free and Independent: The Confederation
   of the United States 1781–1789
James Monroe: Hero of American Diplomacy
The Prodigal Genius: The Life and Times
   of Honoré Balzac
Sad Swashbuckler: The Life
   of William Walker
The Swamp Fox: Biographical Novel
   of General Francis Marion
The Velvet Glove: A Life of Dolly Madison
The Yankee from Tennessee

THE TRIAL OF ANDREW JOHNSON

by NOEL B. GERSON

THOMAS NELSON INC., PUBLISHERS

Nashville   New York

Library of Congress Cataloging in Publication Data

Gerson, Noel Bertram
  The trial of Andrew Johnson.

  Bibliography: p.
  1. Johnson, Andrew, Pres. U. S., 1808-1875—Impeachment.
I. Title.
KF5076.J6G4   353.03′6′0924   76-58489
ISBN 0-8407-6505-3

For
Paul Michael

THE TRIAL OF
ANDREW JOHNSON

At 5 P.M. on Monday, February 24, 1868, members of the United States House of Representatives, exhausted after several days of oratory, began to ballot on an issue unique in the seventy-nine-year history of the Republic under the Constitution. They were voting on the question of whether to impeach Andrew Johnson, seventeenth President of the United States, on thirteen separate charges of having committed high crimes and misdemeanors against the government and the people.

The outcome was taken for granted. Speaker after speaker had denounced the President as a vile, despicable traitor, a villainous conniver who had not only failed to do his duty under the Constitution but also as a man who had led an active conspiracy to destroy the nation. Andrew Johnson's enemies in Washington, who outnumbered his friends overwhelmingly, had done their work well.

The vote was conducted along strict party lines: 126 Republicans voted against the President, whereas 47 Democrats supported him. President Johnson was impeached—that is, formally arraigned. He would next be tried by the United States Senate, with Chief Justice Salmon P. Chase presiding.

The President accepted the news calmly, remarking

that his enemies were causing more problems for themselves than for him.

Around the country, sober-minded citizens were aghast, and even men who had opposed the President were afraid his foes had gone too far. General William T. Sherman, the Union's great war hero, said America would never live down this day of shame. Newspapers in New York, Chicago, and other major northern cities that had attacked Andrew Johnson unmercifully now asked editorially if his foes had gone too far, but it was too late to backtrack now. In Europe, responsible men wondered whether the great American experiment in democracy, seriously damaged by the war that had ended three years earlier, was being destroyed.

Throughout the United States the common people were stunned. Politicians might rant and strike heroic poses, but ordinary men everywhere refused to believe that the President had committed any crimes. He might be headstrong, stubborn, and lacking in tact, but he was one of them, and they knew he loved his country, just as they loved it. His record spoke for itself. No one had suffered more for America, no one had made greater sacrifices for her.

The fifty-nine-year-old President seemed unconcerned about his personal fate. "The Union and the Constitution are in danger," he said, "and I shall continue to defend them, as I have always done, no matter what may happen to me."

Anyone familiar with his background knew he meant every word.

On December 29, 1808, in the little town of Raleigh, North Carolina, a woman known as "Polly" Johnson gave birth to her second son, with her husband, Jacob, in attendance. The place was a one-room squatters' shack, which was all the family could afford. Jacob Johnson was a handyman; his wife took in washing. Both were illiterate.

In later years people said that the couple had named their child after another Carolinian, Andrew Jackson, then a Tennessee lawyer and Indian fighter, but the claim is dubious. The future hero of the Battle of New Orleans, subsequently to become the seventh President of the United States, was still virtually unknown. Andrew Johnson, who would become Jackson's ardent follower, never used a middle name.

Jacob Johnson died when his sons, Bill and Andy, were very small, and his widow was so poor she couldn't afford to erect a headstone over his grave. She struggled hard to eke out a marginal existence, and the little boys ran wild, even when they reached school age. Andrew Johnson never attended any school for as much as a single day in his life.

His mother remarried, but her new husband, a man named Dougherty, was as impoverished as Jacob Johnson had been. In order to provide her children with enough food to remain alive, Polly apprenticed them to a tailor. According to some accounts Andy was ten; other stories say he was thirteen.

No matter what his age, his existence was difficult. Apprentices were bound servants until they reached their majority, and they had as few rights as slaves. Andy worked twelve to fifteen hours a day, seven days a week, and was flogged when he displeased his master. Many years later he indicated he had suffered cruelly during his childhood, but he never discussed the details.

The boy soon demonstrated that he was no ordinary apprentice. He worked hard, without urging, and learned all he could about his craft. He also showed a desire to rise above his station by teaching himself to read, which was a slow, painful, and laborious process. But he persevered, poring over books by candlelight late at night, no matter how weary he was after a long day.

Andy's curiosity was inexhaustible. He pestered literate customers who came to the tailor shop, begging them to show him new words. Several were impressed by his eagerness to learn, his quick mind, and his ability to memorize words at sight. By the time he was fifteen he had taught himself the rudiments of reading.

He was too ambitious to wait another six years before going to work for himself. So he persuaded his brother to accompany him, and they ran away together, setting up a tailor shop of their own in a nearby town. There they prospered for a short time, but their master in Raleigh offered a reward for their capture, and when Andy read the notice, he voluntarily went back to him.

Andy's master refused to take him back. At the same time he vindictively withheld permission for the boy to work in any other tailor shop in the state. So Andy had two choices: Either he could become a handyman like his late father and stepfather, or he could go elsewhere to practice his trade. He chose the latter course, and at the age of sixteen went off on foot across the mountains into the frontier state of Tennessee.

There he lived for brief periods in several communities, and his skill as a tailor, combined with his infinite capacity for hard work, enabled him to earn a living. By coincidence, while he was in the little town of Columbia, he made a new suit for a young lawyer named

James K. Polk. Already showing a strong interest in politics, Polk would become a supporter of Andrew Jackson and eventually the eleventh President of the United States.

By the time Andy Johnson was seventeen, he was fully grown. He was short but broad-shouldered, with a thick torso and a massive head. His hands were small, and his fingertips were callused because of his trade. People said he never started a fight, but they learned not to molest him. When his dark eyes turned black, it was a sign that he had lost his ferocious temper, and he would take on a whole group in a free-for-all fight no matter what the odds against him. Even at this early age he had a reputation for extraordinary personal courage.

After spending a year in Tennessee, where his brother obtained free land and set himself up as a farmer, Andy Johnson returned to North Carolina and brought his mother and stepfather back across the mountains with him to Tennessee. They settled in Greeneville, then the principal community in the eastern part of the state.

Like Andy Johnson, most of the residents were poor whites, hard-working farmers and artisans whose love of freedom bound them together. Slavery flourished elsewhere in Tennessee, but not in the east.

In 1827, prior to his nineteenth birthday, Andy Johnson got married to a girl a year his junior, and for the rest of his days, he said it was the most important thing that ever happened to him. Eliza McCardle was tiny and high-spirited, and she was as ambitious as the young man she married.

Eliza was a schoolteacher, but she gave up her job when she was married, and thereafter she had one pupil, her husband. Thanks to her nightly help Andy Johnson improved his reading, and that was just the beginning. She taught him to write, then taught him arithmetic, history, and geography.

Andy's energies were inexhaustible. He opened his tailor shop at dawn and worked until sundown. At night, with Eliza's help, he studied for long hours, and after he had mastered both reading and writing, he began to collect books. His memory was phenomenal, and he rarely forgot anything he read.

He prospered, carefully saved his money, and built on to the living quarters at the rear of the shop. The Johnsons' first two children, Charles and Martha, were born there.

Andy developed an interest in politics. He served successively as an alderman, as mayor of Greeneville, and as a member of the Tennessee legislature. After that he was sent to Washington as a member of the United States House of Representatives.

From the beginning of his political career Andy Johnson identified with the other poor whites of eastern Tennessee, and he became their spokesman. He achieved such enormous popularity that his enemies, unable to defeat him at the polls, reorganized the state's Congressional districts in order to get rid of him.

Andrew Johnson became a Democrat, at least nominally, not only because it was the party of ordinary citizens and advocated free homesteads and free eduation for all, but because it was the party of his namesake and hero. In 1828, General Jackson was elected to the first of his two terms as President, and young Johnson became one of the lion's devoted cubs.

What a remarkable pack they were! James K. Polk would become President of the United States. Sam Houston would become governor of Tennessee, president of the Republic of Texas, then governor of Texas and United States Senator. Andrew Johnson would become governor of Tennessee, United States Senator, Vice President, and President of the United States.

Jackson's disciples inherited his most cherished convictions, and they never relinquished them. With him they believed the Union was one and indivisible, and that its preservation was a sacred duty. Its principal pillar was the Constitution, which had to be upheld at all costs.

Andrew Johnson became an exceptionally effective orator, because he thoroughly understood his audiences and spoke their language. His voice was deep and mellow, he spoke slowly, and his rhetoric was impassioned, which was typical of his era. He had the ability to inspire large crowds, and although he became increasingly intellectual in his own reading tastes, he took care never to talk above the heads of his audiences.

He became particularly adept in the rough-and-tumble of stump speechmaking. He was quick-witted and fearless, although his sense of humor was limited, and he developed a technique of replying instantly to hecklers, whom he overpowered.

At no time did Johnson become a party adherent in the usual sense. His spirit of independence was too great for that, so he used party politics when it suited his advantage, but went his own way when he wished.

His integrity, like that of Jackson, Polk, and Houston, was phenomenal. When he gave his word to a colleague,

15

he kept it. When he made a deal, he abided by its terms. When he made a campaign promise to the electorate, he went to great lengths to keep that promise.

Above all he was scrupulously honest in his financial dealings. He never accepted a favor, a gift, or a bribe. He and Eliza were frugal and modest and always lived within their means. His greatest extravagance was a walking stick with a small gold-plated handle, which he acquired after he became President. Until he became governor, he was never too proud to work in the tailor shop, and when he served in the House of Representatives, he often spent many hours there on his trips to Greeneville from Washington. He owned the shop until the end of his days, and it was operated for him by an old friend, who became his partner.

The Johnson family continued to grow. A second daughter, Mary, was followed by another son, Robert, and finally there was Andrew, Jr., who was called Frank in the family to avoid confusing him with his father. All of the Johnson children were brought up to live quietly and think twice before spending money.

Nothing better illustrates the frugality of Andrew and Eliza than the financial record they achieved when they lived in the White House during his years as President. The basic expenses of food, servants, and transportation were paid by the government, and Andrew received a salary of $25,000 per year. Out of that he managed to save an average of $17,000 each year. When his political fortunes fell and his enemies, inventing lies with abandon, accused him of accepting graft, he proudly offered to open his personal account books for inspection. He had earned literally every penny of the modest fortune he managed to accumulate.

Eliza played virtually no role in her husband's political life. When Andrew went off to Nashville to serve first in the lower chamber of the legislature, then in the upper, she remained behind in Greeneville with the children. During his ten years as a member of the United States House of Representatives, from 1843 to 1853, Eliza seldom accompanied him to Washington. This was not unusual at the time. Primitive living accommodations in the nation's capital made it necessary for many congressmen and senators to take single lodgings for themselves in boardinghouses.

Martha, who was always her father's favorite, did go to Washington with him in the 1840's, when Polk was President. The First Lady, always interested in the families of the Tennessee delegation, was fond of her, and as a result Martha spent a great deal of time in the White House, where she had the opportunity to watch Sarah Polk superintend the staff, plan state dinners, and act as her husband's hostess. This experience would prove exceptionally valuable after Andrew Johnson became President, because although Eliza accompanied her husband to Washington and lived in the White House, her health was frail and she rarely appeared at official functions. Instead Martha, herself married to a senator and the mother of several children, acted as her father's hostess.

When Andrew Johnson was elected governor of Tennessee in 1853, the entire family accompanied him to Nashville, but neither Eliza nor the children liked the Governor's Mansion, and found reasons to spend long periods in Greeneville.

Johnson was enormously popular with his constituents when he was a congressman, and the whole state idolized him throughout both of his two-year terms as governor. Not only did the common man identify with him, but men of every political persuasion applauded his rugged independence. Andy Johnson voted and acted in accordance with his own conscience, and although nominally a Democrat, he voted with the Whigs when he thought they were right.

No President could force or cajole him into line, no party leader could apply pressure to him successfully. He was the champion of free public education for all, and insisted that the issue transcended party lines. "Children don't care if we're Democrats or Whigs, or belong to any other party," he said after he became governor. "They deserve the chance to read and write, and it is the obligation of every public officeholder to give them that chance. I'll campaign against any man who votes against free education!"

In 1855, when campaigning for his second term as governor of Tennessee, Andrew Johnson demonstrated his personal brand of courage in a gesture that made him an overnight hero to decent law-abiding men everywhere in the United States. He was opposed by a candidate nominated by the self-styled American Party, more commonly called the Know-Nothings. This group, which was opposed to immigration and had a violent anti-Catholic bias, based its appeal on secrecy and terror.

In a major speech before an audience composed in large part of Know-Nothing sympathizers, Johnson attacked the party as an organization of bigots, unprincipled and shameless, and he proposed that they be outlawed. Many in his audience were outraged, and it appeared they might mob him, but he stared them down.

Later that same day a delegation called on Governor Johnson and warned him that if he launched another attack on the Know-Nothings he would be shot. He listened, smiled, and made no comment.

A few days later Johnson was scheduled to make another address, and by coincidence he was speaking in a Know-Nothing stronghold. Friends and supporters urged him to cancel the engagement, but he refused, and he would not allow a bodyguard to accompany him. Under no circumstances, he said, would he allow himself to be intimidated.

A silent crowd watched him grimly as he walked alone through the hall to the rostrum. Then, as the audience looked on in astonishment, he took a pistol from his pocket and placed it on the lectern. "Fellow citizens," he said, "it is proper when free men assemble for the discussion of important public matters that everything should be done decently and in order. I have been informed that part of the business to be transacted on the present occasion is the assassination of the individual who now has the honor of addressing you. If any man has come here for the purpose indicated, I do not say to him, let him speak, *but let him shoot.*"

His right hand curled around the butt of his pistol, and his index finger found the trigger.

There was an electric silence, and no one in the audience moved.

"Gentlemen," Governor Johnson said calmly, "it appears that I have been misinformed. I will now proceed to address you on the subject that has called us together."

He made his speech, vigorously attacking the Know-Nothings. When he was finished, he put away his pistol and walked unmolested from the hall.

Newspapers throughout the United States played up the story, and the Know-Nothings lost influence everywhere. Governor Johnson was reelected by an overwhelming majority of Tennesseans, and for all practical purposes he and his followers assumed complete control of the state. The Know-Nothings were smashed, the Whigs were inconsequential, and the Democrats, if they hoped to survive politically, were forced to jump on the Johnson bandwagon.

While he was governor, both of his daughters were married. Mary became the wife of Daniel Stover, a prosperous eastern Tennessee farmer, and Martha was married to Circuit Judge David T. Patterson of Greeneville, a staunch Johnson supporter. Both of the young wives soon began to rear families of their own.

In 1857, at the conclusion of his second term as governor, Andrew Johnson returned to the national scene as United States Senator from Tennessee.

The slavery question, including the issue of the expansion of slavery to territories that ultimately would become states, had become paramount, almost to the exclusion of other matters. President James Buchanan was an amiable man, who was subsequently blamed for his inability to prevent the deepening schism that separated North and South. Perhaps posterity has judged him too severely; it is unlikely that any President could have prevented the cleavage.

As a senator from a slaveholding state, Andrew Johnson was automatically expected to support the positions taken by the South. But, as always, he had his own ideas. He was the only senator from the South who supported free homestead bills in the developing territories. His colleagues opposed such policies because the lure of free land would send many settlers from the North into these areas, and ultimately their votes would be cast against the extension of slavery. In Johnson's opinion it was far more important that every citizen be given the opportunity to improve his lot.

In one point he agreed with others from the South. He was opposed to the Abolitionists who wanted to do away with the entire institution of slavery, but his reasons were his own. Eventually, he believed, slavery would wither away. But immediate and total abolition would cause a severe economic wrench, and he criticized the Abolitionists because they offered no practical solution to this problem. In his opinion they were troublemakers, and he was convinced that if hotheads on both sides of the issue kept silent, passions would cool, and reasonable, moderate men of good faith would have greater opportunities to work out solutions satisfactory to everyone.

As the nation drifted closer and closer to the tragedy of civil war, Senator Johnson stood apart from his Southern colleagues, many of whom began to speak of forming a new nation to be called the Confederacy. The association of the states in one nation, under the Constitution, could not be dissolved, he argued. The compact that had created the United States was sacred.

Again and again he quoted his idol, President Andrew Jackson: "The Union must and shall be preserved."

He was also opposed to efforts being made by Northern senators to diminish the rights of the South under the Constitution, and he was painfully candid, in speech after speech, when he declared that slavery existed in the North as well as in the South. In the latter region, it was black, while in the factories and industrial plants of the North, it was white. Slavery, he insisted, had many guises.

When fellow Democrats tried to persuade him to line up with the party on such issues as the establishment of a railroad across the continent, Johnson announced in a speech, "I am no party man, bound by no party platform, and will vote as I please."

He crossed swords frequently with a colleague from Mississippi, Jefferson Davis. Their disputes, based largely on personality, arose from the differences in their social backgrounds. Davis was a patrician, Johnson, a plebian, a "poor white," and their approaches to life were very different. Neither had any idea that the day would come when Johnson, as President of the United States, would be forced to decide whether to try Davis, as the former President of the Confederacy, for his life, or to pardon him.

As the North became more virulent in the passage of legislation that curbed the South, Southern senators sought ways to avoid their constitutional responsibilities. Johnson would not tolerate such activities. "Because we cannot get our constitutional rights," he said, "I do not intend to be one of those who violate the Constitution. I intend to place myself on the Constitution which I have sworn to support, and to stand there and battle for all its guarantees."

Southern colleagues began to snub Johnson when it appeared that he was friendly with such Northerners as William Henry Seward of New York and the fire-eating, antislavery zealot Benjamin Franklin Wade. Seward, a distinguished attorney, was being mentioned as a possible candidate for President. Wade, one of the few men in America who was as effective a stump speaker as Andrew Johnson, was also a product of the rough-and-tumble school of politics, and the two men developed a grudging respect for each other.

Seward and Wade were destined to play prominent roles in the climactic chapter of Johnson's career. The former would serve President Abraham Lincoln as Secretary of State and, retained in that post by Johnson, would act as his faithful, level-headed counselor. Wade's part would be even more dramatic. As president *pro tempore*, or temporary, of the Senate, he would stand next in line for the Presidency of the United States in the event that Johnson was thrown out of office. But in 1858, of course, none of the principal players in that future drama had any notion of what lay in store.

As the Democratic convention of 1860 approached, Andrew Johnson was mentioned as a possible candidate for the Presidency, but he decried his own chances. Stephen A. Douglas of Illinois was the Democratic favorite, and although Johnson disliked him personally, he was content with the party's choice. He knew most of his fellow Southerners would not give him their support because of his rugged independence.

Whatever chance Johnson might have had of winning the nomination evaporated when he made a typically blunt statement, in which he condemned Abolitionist Massachusetts and slaveholding champion South Carolina in the same breath. "I would chain Massachusetts and South Carolina together," he declared, "and I would transport them to some island in the Arctic Ocean, the colder the better, till they cool off and come to their senses."

Other men feared that the Union would be dissolved, but Johnson was unable to share their pessimistic view.

The Union was a solid rock that ordinary mortals could not shatter, and soon even the most outspoken advocates of secession would come to their senses. As he later admitted, he was being naïve. His own devotion to his country and the Constitution were so great he found it impossible to believe that others were sincere when they swore they would break up the Union rather than allow the South to be deprived of her rights.

The Democrats were so badly split that they could not agree on a candidate for President. The Northern wing of the party nominated Douglas, while the Southerners named Buchanan's Vice-President, John C. Breckinridge of Kentucky.

Meanwhile, the new Republican party, which met in Chicago, nominated Abraham Lincoln of Illinois. The South hated him so passionately that many of her leaders, including members of the Senate, openly predicted that the whole region would secede if he was elected.

In the months immediately preceding the election of 1860, it finally dawned on Andrew Johnson that the South meant what it said. If Lincoln should be elected, eleven states would secede.

He made his own position clear, announcing, "When the crisis comes, I will be found standing by the Union."

A few days later he amplified that statement, saying he would "return to Washington and come out distinctly in opposition to a dissolution of the Union. The attempt to secede will fail, as the South has no resources, cannot manufacture arms, and will probably be cut off from the whole world. Slavery will find no friends anywhere."

Most men of political prominence in Tennessee disagreed with Johnson and tried to persuade him to change. Lincoln, if elected, would represent only the

North and would not be President of the South. A man's first loyalties lay with his state, Tennessee, and thereafter with his region, the South.

Johnson regarded such talk as gibberish. He was a citizen of the United States of America. He had taken an oath to uphold her Constitution, and this he would do, regardless of the consequences, political or personal. He could not be moved.

Only one other Southern leader felt as Johnson did, and it was not accidental that the man was another of Andrew Jackson's lion cubs. General Sam Houston, president of Texas when she had been a republic, until recently one of her United States senators and now her governor, was voicing the same sentiments in the same terms. "The Union must be preserved," he roared. "Secession is treason."

His Southern compatriots would not listen to him any more than they would listen to Andrew Johnson.

2

Abraham Lincoln was elected sixteenth President of the United States in November 1860. The Congress reconvened early in December, and Senator Andrew Johnson of Tennessee listened as his Southern colleagues predicted that their states would secede before Lincoln was inaugurated. Johnson knew that slavery alone was not the issue. The South had controlled the nation since the Republic had been founded, but now, thanks to immigration from Europe and rapid industrialization, the larger, wealthier, and more heavily populated North was becoming dominant.

In an attempt to obtain a fair balance between the sections, he proposed several amendments to the Constitution, among them a proposal that the President and Vice President be elected by direct, popular vote, and that one come from a free state and the other from a slave state.

However, it was too late for compromises, and Johnson's ideas were ignored. The temper of the times demanded action.

Various senators made speeches outlining the stands taken by their states and making their own positions clear. On December 18, 1860, it was Andrew Johnson's turn, and the galleries were filled as he delivered one of his most succinct, stirring orations. He said, in part:

27

We are now involved in a revolution. I think it behooves every man . . . to indicate, in some manner, his opinions and sentiments in reference to the questions that agitate and distract the public mind. I shall be very frank. . . . I am opposed to secession. I believe it is no remedy for the evils complained of. . . . I believe that this battle should be fought not outside, but inside of the Union, and upon the battlements of the Constitution itself.

I believe it is the imperative duty of Congress to make some effort to save the country from impending dissolution; and he that is unwilling to make an effort to preserve the Constitution and the Union . . . I think is unworthy of public confidence and the respect . . . of the American people.

We do not intend to leave the Union. We do not intend to go out. It is our Constitution. It is our Union, and we do not intend to be driven from it.

If the doctrine of secession is to be carried out upon the mere whim of a state, this government is at an end. It is not stronger than a rope of sand; its own weight will tumble it to pieces. If a state may secede at will and pleasure, why, I ask you, on the other hand, as Madison asks, cannot a majority of the states combine and reject a state out of the Confederacy? There is but one way to get out of the Union without the consent of the parties, and that is by revolution. . . .

What is the issue? It is not slavery, but this and this only: we have not got our man. If we had got our man, we should not be for breaking up the Union. . . .

Let South Carolina send her senators back, and on the fourth of March next we will have a majority of six in this body. . . . Mr. Lincoln cannot make his cabinet . . . unless the Senate will permit him. He cannot send a foreign minister or even a consul abroad, if the Senate be unwilling. He cannot even appoint a postmaster. . . . I voted against him. I spoke against him. I spent my money to defeat him. But I still love my country. I love the Constitution. I intend to insist upon its guarantees. There, and there alone, I intend to plant myself. . . .

Let us show ourselves men, and men of courage. . . . We have it in our power—yes, this Congress today has it in its power to save the Union. . . . Shall we shrink from our duty and desert the government as a sinking ship, or shall we stand by it? . . . The time has come when men should speak out. Duties are mine; consequences are God's. I intend to do my duty!

The Constitution declares and defines what is treason. Let us talk about things by their right name! . . . If anything be treason, is not levying war upon the United States treason? Is not attempt to take its property treason? It is treason, and nothing but treason, and if one state, upon its own volition, can go out of this Confederacy without regard to the effect it is to have upon the remaining parties to the compact, what is your government worth? It is no government at all! . . .

I believe there is too much good sense, too much intelligence, too much patriotism, too much capability, too much virtue in the great mass of people to permit the government to be overthrown. I have an abiding faith, I have an unshaken confidence in man's capability to govern himself. I will not give up this government. No, I intend to stand by it, and I entreat every man throughout the nation who is a patriot to rally around the altar of our common country, and swear by our God that the Constitution shall be saved and the Union preserved.

I intend to stand by the Constitution as it is, insisting upon a compliance with its guarantees. I intend to stand by it as the sheer anchor of the government; and I trust and hope, though it seems to be now in the very vortex of ruin, that it will be preserved, and will remain a beacon to guide, and an example to be imitated by all the nations of the earth. Yes, I intend to hold on to it as the chief ark of our safety, as the palladium of our civil and our religious liberty. I intend to cling to it as the shipwrecked mariner clings to the last plank, when the night and the tempest close around him. It is the last hope of human freedom.

In saying what I have said, Mr. President, I have done it in view of the duty that I felt I owed to my constituents, to my children, to myself. Without regard to the consequences I have taken my position; and when the tug comes . . . then it is that I will perish in the last breach; yes, in the language of the patriot Emmett, "I will dispute every inch of ground; and I will burn every blade of grass; and the last entrenchment of freedom shall be in my grave." Then let us stand by the Constitution; and, in saving the Union, save this, the greatest government on earth.

Other senators had delivered more polished, more intellectual speeches since the foundation of the Republic. None had ever spoken with greater sincerity. That address was the crystallization of Andrew Johnson's most cherished convictions. More than anything else he ever said or wrote, it explains the depth of his feeling when he was impeached. Then, as on the eve of the Civil War, he was not concerned about what might become of him. He was fighting for the Constitution and the preservation of the Union. He was fighting for freedom, which meant more to him than life itself.

His speech created a sensation. Northern senators shook his hand, but he was indifferent to their praise. Southern senators ignored him, but he was impervious to their snubs. Northern newspapers hailed him as a great patriot; Southern newspapers denounced him as a traitor.

Tennessee, a border state where men of both persuasions lived side by side, was bewildered. Johnson, the most popular man Tennessee had known since Andrew Jackson, had taken an unequivocal stand in favor of the Union. Thousands were influenced by him, but other thousands turned away from him. His address solved no problems, but merely clarified the issues.

The speech was significant because it had been delivered by a Southerner, and the demand for copies was almost as great in the South as in the North. Johnson himself paid for fifteen thousand copies, and large numbers were ordered by the Chattanooga *Gazette* and other newspapers. More than anything Andrew Johnson had ever said or done, his December speech brought him to national prominence.

But nothing now could prevent the states of the South from leaving the Union. South Carolina was the first to secede, on December 20, 1860, punctuating her action two weeks later, when the state's cannon drove off a supply ship, the *Star of the West*, which was carrying provisions to the Federal garrison at Fort Sumter in Charleston Harbor. Before January ended Mississippi, Alabama, Florida, Georgia, and Louisiana had seceded. They were followed by Texas on February 1. Governor Houston refused to take the oath that required him to support the Confederacy. "I stand for the Union and the Constitution," he said, and was promptly deposed. He returned to his home, and so great was his prestige that no man dared to lay a hand on him.

Senator Jefferson Davis, who would become President of the Confederate States of America before the end of the month, made a farewell address to his colleagues, during which he viciously attacked Ben Wade and called Andrew Johnson a Judas.

A plebiscite was ordered in Tennessee, the first state to submit the question of secession to an election. The date was February 9. Johnson's duties required him to remain in Washington, but he made several more speeches in the same vein as his stirring December address, and they were duly reported at length in the major Tennessee newspapers. So great was his prestige that even those papers favoring secession felt obliged to print his words.

On February 9, the voters of Tennessee went to the polls, where they firmly rejected a call to a convention that would have taken the state out of the Union. For the moment, at least, Tennessee remained in the fold. Men inside and outside the state gave full credit to Andrew Johnson.

Senator Johnson attended the inauguration of President Lincoln, but made no public comments about the event.

On April 12, Fort Sumter was bombarded by South Carolina troops, and the Federal garrison was forced to surrender. The Civil War had started, and President Lincoln issued a proclamation in which he declared that a state of insurrection existed in the states that had seceded. Nevertheless four more states seceded during April and May: Virginia, Arkansas, Tennessee, and North Carolina.

Governor Isham Harris of Tennessee, an ardent advocate of secession, had ignored the results of the February plebiscite and ordered the legislature to meet in a special session for the purpose of taking the state out of the Union. Senator Johnson was inundated with telegrams and letters from friends and other Union supporters, begging him to return home without delay. Only he could turn the tide.

He heeded the call, departing from Washington late in April. His train had to travel through Virginia, which had recently seceded, and angry mobs gathered at various stops. Johnson appeared on the platform at each station, and when one man brandished a pistol, he drew his own. However, the Confederates were taking no unnecessary risks, and several stops were avoided when it became obvious that the menace to the senator's safety was too great. Tennessee was still teetering on the brink, and could fall into either camp. If Confederate zealots murdered Andrew Johnson, he would become a martyr in his own state, which undoubtedly would remain in the Union. The senator reached home without further trouble.

Eastern Tennessee was strongly Unionist in sentiment, but elsewhere the Confederacy was favored, and most Democrats; including men who had been Andrew Johnson's ardent supporters, were now outspoken on behalf of the Rebel cause.

Showing no fear, no concern for his own life, Johnson plunged into the struggle and stumped the state. When Confederate partisans tried to silence him by raising rifles and pistols, he drew his own pistol. He demanded—and was granted—the right to be heard. Only his incredible personal courage saved him. Again and again he was threatened, but he refused to desist.

No man laid a hand on Johnson as he traveled through the state. Like Sam Houston in Texas, he had such great stature and displayed such bravery that he was safe. Friends described him as cool, eloquent, and determined; even his enemies were impressed. He was accompanied by representatives of newspapers from both the Union and the Confederacy, and there was a note of awe in their stories. The man literally didn't understand the meaning of fear.

As the preelection hysteria mounted, wild stories began to circulate. Louisiana was sending two thousand militiamen into Tennessee to capture Andrew Johnson. A band of Confederates from Nashville planned to assassinate him. Three hired killers had set out from Memphis, intending to shoot him on sight. Friends repeatedly begged him to leave the state before it was too late. Andrew Johnson refused and continued to take the stump.

On June 8, Tennessee went to the polls to elect new members of the legislature who would either keep the state in the Union or join the Confederacy. The tide of popular feeling had turned, and only in eastern Tennessee, Johnson's stronghold, was the Union favored by a 2 to 1 vote. Elsewhere the vote was 2 to 1 in favor of secession.

Ordinary prudence required Senator Johnson to leave Tennessee before she formally joined the Confederacy. He said good-bye to his wife, children, and grandchildren, and leaving all of his possessions behind except for a change of clothing, he departed. A Confederate colonel had given the order to halt "the traitor Johnson," and the senator was urged to go in disguise. But he replied that it would be cowardly to sneak away.

Instead, accompanied by three friends, he rode in a

small, open carriage. He was seen by literally thousands of militiamen who had already taken the Confederate oath, and certainly he was the best-known, most widely recognized of Tennessee's sons.

Not one roadblock was erected, not one rifle was raised to stop him, and many of the militiamen saluted as he passed. Nevertheless, the danger was very real that some rabid Confederate partisan might try to gain some small measure of immortality by shooting him.

He spent two days and nights traveling through the mountains, and finally reached Kentucky. That border state was wavering, too, so Union adherents arranged a major rally in Louisville, and Johnson addressed a cheering crowd of thousands. Rightly or wrongly, he was given credit for keeping Kentucky in the Union. A similar reception awaited him in Cincinnati, which also gave him a hero's welcome. In both cities, however, there were many Southern sympathizers, and in spite of his protests, strong bodyguards were assigned to protect him. A group of heavily armed men accompanied him on board the train that took him to Washington, too.

In all, eleven states joined the Confederacy, and twenty-one of their twenty-two Senators joined the newly created nation. Only Andrew Johnson remained loyal to the Union.

As soon as he reached Washington, he was summoned by President Lincoln. He spent an entire afternoon at the White House, discussing the state of affairs in Tennessee with the President. This was the first time the two men talked to each other in depth. Both were members of the poor-white class, both had risen from humble origins, both were imbued with a frontier mentality.

Each took the other's measure, and each was impressed. They established a cordial rapport that lasted until President Lincoln's tragic assassination.

Both men recognized the importance of Tennessee as a corridor between the eastern and western states of the Confederacy, and had the Federals moved swiftly, they might have regained control of the state, particularly since there were so many Union sympathizers in the eastern part. But the North was slow in organizing its war effort, and the Confederacy, wasting no time, sent thousands of troops into the state. The Union would have to take it by force of arms.

Charles and Robert Johnson, the senator's elder sons, managed to join the United States Army and obtain commissions, the former as a colonel and regimental commander. Dan Stover, Mary's husband, also was awarded a colonelcy. Eliza Johnson and her youngest son, her daughters, and their children continued to live in their own homes behind Confederate lines, and were treated courteously. The suggestion that they be taken into custody and held as prisoners was brusquely rejected by a Confederate brigadier general, who said, "We don't make war on women and children." Andrew Johnson may have been regarded as an apostate, but Southern gallantry protected his family.

As the war progressed, however, the family's situation deteriorated. Judge Patterson, doubly prominent as Johnson's son-in-law and as a staunch Union supporter, was arrested and sent to prison for an indefinite term, presumably for the duration of the war. Governor Harris was under pressure from his own supporters, and as a consequence, confiscated the Johnson house and the tailor shop in Greeneville. This forced Mrs. Johnson and Frank to take refuge with Martha Patterson.

The worst of the situation was that the senator and his wife could no longer communicate with each other by letter or telegraph. Occasionally a Loyalist refugee from eastern Tennessee arrived in Washington, bringing the senator word that the members of his family were alive and well, but Mrs. Johnson received no word of him, and her problem was complicated by the many unsubstantiated rumors that appeared in various Confederate newspapers. One said he had been killed in Kentucky, another that he had been gravely wounded in Washington. It was impossible for her to obtain confirmation or denial of these lies, and she suffered intensely.

Johnson busied himself looking after the interests of Tennessee. Thanks to his efforts, large supplies of arms and ammunition were smuggled into the state and handed over to Union partisans. And he was indefatigable in looking after the interests of the refugees who escaped across the mountains into Union territory.

The Senate began to debate on the purpose of the war, and the discussion intensified after the severe loss the Federals suffered in the Battle of Bull Run. Andrew Johnson, true to the principles that had guided him for so many years, submitted a simple resolution. He wanted the restoration of the Union, as it had been prior to the war, under an unchanged Constitution.

The vote in favor of his resolution was almost unanimous. Only Senator Charles Sumner of Massachusetts abstained. It was his view that the sole purpose of the war was to crush the rebellious states.

An identical resolution was introduced in the House of

Representatives by John J. Crittenden of Kentucky, a former Secretary of State who had also served as governor and senator. Two votes were cast against the resolution in the House, one by Congressman Thaddeus Stevens of Pennsylvania. His aim, like that of Sumner, was to grind the South into submission and transform it into a colony of the North.

Johnson answered these vengeful radical Republicans from the Senate floor in a speech that created a sensation throughout the North. It was one of his most statesmanlike efforts, and its climax was reprinted by scores of newspapers. He said:

> Let partisan politics be forgotten. I am a Democrat today. I expect to die one. But do not talk about Republicans now; do not talk about Democrats; do not talk about Whigs or Know-Nothings now; talk about your country and the Constitution and the Union. Save that; preserve the integrity of the government; once more place it erect among the nations of the earth; and then, if we want to divide about questions that may arise in our midst, we have a government to divide in.
>
> Though the government has met with a little reverse within a short distance of this city, no one should be discouraged. Let the energies of the government be redoubled and let it go on with the war . . . not a war upon sections, not a war upon peculiar institutions anywhere, but let the Constitution be its frontispiece, and the supremacy and enforcement of the laws its watchword. Then it can, it will, go on triumphantly.
>
> We must succeed. This government must not, cannot fail. Though your flag may have trailed in the dust, though a retrograde movement may have been made, though the banner of our country may have been sullied, let it be borne onward. And if, for the prosecution of this

war in behalf of the government and the Constitution, it is necessary to cleanse and purify that banner, I say let it be baptized in fire from the sun and bathed in a nation's blood! The nation must be redeemed! It must be triumphant! The Constitution—which is based upon principles immutable and upon which rest the rights of men and the hopes and expectations of those who love freedom throughout the civilized world—must be maintained!

Volunteer recruits flocked to the standard of the United States Army after the speech was published. Former Senator Alexander H. Stephens of Georgia, now Vice President of the Confederacy, estimated that Johnson's address was responsible for an increase of at least a hundred thousand in the ranks of Federals. When a delegation of senators and congressmen called at the White House to discuss economic, political, and military developments in the struggle, President Lincoln turned to Senator Johnson and publicly called him one of the Union's greatest assets.

Late in the autumn of 1861, during a Congressional recess, Johnson went to Ohio, where he made a number of speeches before large crowds. He was taken to a military camp where two thousand men, refugees from eastern Tennessee like himself, were in training. He was scheduled to address them, but was so overcome by emotion that he couldn't say a single word. Instead he "disgraced" himself by weeping.

After Congress reconvened, Johnson became one of eight members of the new Joint Committee on the Conduct of the War, a watchdog group formed for the purpose of taking all steps necessary to ensure a Union victory. Ben Wade was the chairman, and his relations with his colleague from Tennessee were cordial. They dined together frequently, as each was living alone in Washington, and one day Senator Wade paid his colleague the greatest compliment he was capable of uttering. "Senator Johnson may be a Democrat," he declared, "but first and foremost he is a patriot. Would that we had more like him in this chamber." In a few years those sentiments would be forgotten.

Early in 1862, Johnson finally had some direct family news from Robert. Judge Patterson had been released from prison, but had been arrested again after refusing to take an oath that would have prohibited him from acting on behalf of the Union. His continuing imprisonment embarrassed the Confederates, however, so he had again been released and had rejoined his family. Mrs. Johnson and Frank currently were living with Mary Stover, whose husband's regiment was engaging in guerrilla warfare against the Rebels, as was Charles Johnson's unit. Robert himself had narrowly escaped capture during a skirmish, and said the Confederates would have hanged him if they had caught him. "I would have been their substitute for you," he wrote. In a postscript, he said the Johnson house in Greeneville was being used as a Confederate army hospital.

Late in February 1862, Robert arrived in Washington and was reunited with his father. Secretary of War Edwin Stanton promptly granted him a commission as a colonel and authorized him to raise a regiment of Tennessee volunteers.

A new Federal general who had appeared in the West, Ulysses S. Grant, was winning victories in Tennessee, and the improvement in the military situation there caused President Lincoln to think in terms of bringing the state into the Union fold. He believed that only one man was capable of performing this feat, and his principal advisers, Secretary of State Seward and Secretary of War Stanton, agreed with him.

Lincoln invited Andrew Johnson to the White House and asked if he would be willing to give up his Senate seat in order to become military governor of Tennessee. Without an instant's hesitation Johnson accepted.

Federal troops had occupied Nashville and a small area around it. Thereafter, they would try to broaden their base and gradually take possession of the entire state. Johnson's task would be difficult. He would be in personal danger, too, as there were many Rebel sympathizers in Nashville.

In addition to his title as military governor, he was also given a commission as a brigadier general in the United States Army. He did not regard himself as a soldier in any sense, but the President thought the commission would make it easier for him to deal with rank-conscious generals and colonels. He was given extraordinary powers and was responsible only to Lincoln.

Johnson's appointment, for which there was no precedent in American history, became effective on March 3, 1862, and he left Washington that same day for Nashville. Traveling by way of Cincinnati, he arrived on March 12.

A few days later he issued a proclamation that expressed the philosophy on which he and President Lincoln were in complete agreement. He came to Tennessee as a peacemaker and urged all citizens loyal to the Union to join with him in the restoration of order. He would engage in no reprisals for illegal acts perpetrated by Confederates, but treason would be punished severely, and those who persisted in their opposition to the United

States would have cause to regret it. However, any Rebel sympathizer who recanted and mended his ways would be granted a full, complete amnesty.

In this proclamation Johnson emphasized a point that was the keystone of his convictions: Tennessee had never left the Union, because no state had the right to secede.

Early in April General Grant won the Battle of Shiloh, and later in the month New Orleans fell to the Federal navy. The Confederates were forced to withdraw from all of Tennessee except the eastern portion of the state, which they placed under martial law.

Eliza Johnson was ordered to evacuate without delay, but the strain of her precarious existence had taken its toll, and she was too ill to travel. Because of her condition she was granted one delay after another.

Governor Johnson was eager to see a Federal army take eastern Tennessee, but the troops were needed elsewhere, so he concentrated on returning the region under his control to normal. Farmers were encouraged to plant crops, and cotton buyers from the North swarmed to the state. County courts were reopened, with their judges appointed by Governor Johnson. The presence of Federal troops made travel by road and by water relatively safe.

Daily living was anything but easy or pleasant for Andrew Johnson. He was eager to be reunited with his wife and daughters and, knowing nothing of Eliza's illness, couldn't understand why she did not come through the lines to join him. He worked seven days and seven nights a week, often remaining at his desk for eighteen hours at a stretch and sometimes sleeping on a cot in his office. A number of young Confederates threatened to assassinate him, and his life was in constant danger. Rebel sympathizers, from minor officials who refused to take an oath of loyalty to the Union to clergymen who preached pro-Confederate sermons, had to be ferreted out.

Many of Nashville's more prominent citizens snubbed him, but their attitude was the least of his worries. "Aristocrats and I have never had much sociability together," he said. "Oil and water still don't mix."

In an attempt to rekindle enthusiasm for the Union cause, Johnson did what came naturally and took to the stump. Military men were alarmed, afraid he would either be murdered or kidnapped by Confederates, but he persisted. He traveled to many towns and made many addresses. Others were relieved whenever he returned safely to Nashville, but he was always cool, seemingly at ease.

On a number of occasions Confederate armies pushed into Tennessee, and late in July 1862 a Rebel column reached a point only six miles from the capital. Johnson promptly demonstrated his courage. He not only refused to evacuate, but sent word to the enemy that rather than surrender Nashville, he would burn it to the ground. The Confederates knew him well enough to realize he wasn't bluffing, and retreated.

Robert Johnson, whose regiment was operating near the Rebel lines in eastern Tennessee, managed to obtain word that his mother had been ill, but that her health was improving. He sent a telegram to his father, who was temporarily relieved.

In September 1862, Nashville faced a crisis. A strong Confederate force under General Nathan Bedford Forrest besieged the city and managed to surround it. Governor Johnson vowed that he would never surrender, and the drama gripped people on both sides.

One month after the siege began, Eliza Johnson arrived outside Nashville, and General Forrest gallantly allowed her and her family to pass through the Confederate lines. She was accompanied by Frank, as well as by Mary Stover and her three small children. Colonel Dan Stover and Colonel Charles Johnson had materialized, seemingly out of nowhere, as escorts for the women and children. General Forrest chivalrously refused to detain either of these Federal officers.

The joy of the reunion of Andrew Johnson with his wife, children, and grandchildren was great. Martha Patterson, her husband, and their two children were still in Greeneville, and Robert was on duty near the Cumberland Gap, but all the rest of the family were together at last.

Military Governor Johnson celebrated by announcing that Nashville would hold out, and the siege dragged on.

Early in November a Federal relief force commanded by General William S. Rosecrans pushed southward from Kentucky and approached the city. Forrest redoubled his efforts to take Nashville.

Andrew Johnson, busily preparing the defenses at the capitol, issued only one public statement: "I am no military man, but anyone who talks of surrendering I will shoot!"

Then the Federal army won a decisive victory, at Corinth, Mississippi, and the Confederates were compelled to withdraw. On November 14 General Rosecrans entered Nashville, bringing the siege to an end.

Governor Johnson returned to the task of trying to reunite the people of the war-torn state.

The influence his wife exerted was noted by everyone who came in contact with the governor, especially the members of his staff. Previously he had been harsh, blunt, and caustic in his personal dealings with Confederate sympathizers. Now he treated them with quiet good humor, showed sympathy for them, and even urged his subordinates to "use sugar instead of vinegar."

In January 1863, President Lincoln issued his Emancipation Proclamation, which freed the slaves in territories still controlled by the Confederates. His primary aim, of course, was the disruption of the Rebel economy. Certain sections were exempted, among them Tennessee, at Governor Johnson's request. The freeing of the slaves created as many problems as it solved, among them the pressing question of how these new freedmen would live, and Johnson, who knew that even the most loyal of Tennessee Unionists would be split, wanted to wait until the state itself voted slavery out of existence.

His good faith cannot be questioned. A decade earlier he had himself purchased several slaves, and he now owned eight. When the Emancipation Proclamation was issued, he not only gave them their freedom instantly, but continued to provide for them. Later, after the Johnsons returned to Greeneville, he hired the head of the black family to work in his tailor shop, scrupulously paying him wages equal to those of his white foreman.

In 1863, Governor Johnson gradually adopted an increasingly stern attitude toward Confederate sympathizers who refused to take an oath of loyalty. At the very least their property was confiscated. Those who were suspected of dealing with the enemy were imprisoned.

In the spring, Charles Johnson, who had survived many months of guerrilla warfare, was killed when he was thrown by a high-spirited horse. He had been Eliza's favorite, and the tragedy crushed her. Martha Patterson later said that her mother never completely recovered from the blow.

Colonel Stover insisted on returning to duty with his regiment, even though the privations he had suffered when waging guerrilla warfare had caused him to contract tuberculosis. He remained in the field until he became so ill that he was returned to Nashville on a litter, and there he died in his wife's arms.

In spite of these personal losses, Governor Johnson never slackened his pace. Not only did he continue to work sixteen to eighteen hours each day, but he unfailingly responded to requests from other states to address patriotic rallies. He traveled to Kentucky, Illinois, Indiana, and Ohio, and promised to speak later in New York, New Jersey, Maryland, and Pennsylvania.

He had become an important national figure, but he and Eliza continued to live modestly. When one of his granddaughters wanted to buy a pony, the governor rebuked her: "We're poor people, and we can't afford such fripperies. What's more, there are people in this country who are starving, and it would be sinful to waste money on luxuries. In our family, we don't ride. We walk!"

In the summer of 1863, the Federals began to plan in earnest for the conquest of eastern Tennessee, and President Lincoln summoned Governor Johnson to take part in the discussions. While in Washington, Johnson not only saw the President daily, but renewed his friendship with members of the Committee on the Conduct of the

War. On at least two evenings, he and Ben Wade dined together.

He was in the capital on July 4, when the Federals won their two greatest victories to date. General Grant captured Vicksburg, where he accepted the surrender of more than thirty thousand Confederates. And in Pennsylvania, at what came to be known as the Battle of Gettysburg, Confederate General Robert E. Lee was defeated after a bold attempt to invade the North. The losses on both sides were staggering, and Andrew Johnson shared the sorrow of President Lincoln and other compassionate, thinking men.

There was no longer any real doubt that the Confederates ultimately would be defeated, and Johnson was sickened by the attitude of the radical Republicans, who gloated in Senate and House speeches as they recounted Confederate losses.

"The dead on both sides are Americans," a somber Johnson wrote to his wife. "One day, and may it come soon, we will be reunited under one flag and one Constitution. We are still brothers, and that brotherhood will be reaffirmed. I grieve for every Confederate mother and father who have lost a son, just as I weep for every Union parent who has been bereaved. May this terrible slaughter soon end."

This letter was strictly private, not intended for publication or other political purposes, and expressed Andrew Johnson's deepest convictions. In fact, the letter did not come to light until early in the twentieth century, more than fifty years after his death.

In spite of these sentiments, however, he cracked down hard on the disloyal after his return to Tennessee. To do otherwise, he believed, would prolong the war and the suffering, and lengthen the lists of dead and wounded on both sides. "The end is in sight," he said in an address to Rebels after his return to Nashville. "We extend a hand to you. Join with us in the sanctuary of the Union, under the protection of the Constitution. Refuse at your peril! We offer you brotherhood or the sword. There are no other choices."

In August 1863, the Federals opened their campaign for eastern Tennessee, and on September 2 Knoxville fell to a Federal column. Within a few days the Confederates had fled, and Andrew Johnson's domain was reunited.

The victory was short-lived. The Confederates rallied, Chattanooga was threatened, and the Federal center in Tennessee was in danger of collapse. The military high command was reorganized, with General Grant given the supreme command in the western theater of operations. By the end of November, the Battles of Missionary Ridge and Lookout Mountain had been fought, and the Rebels were driven from the state.

At last Tennessee was ready for the complete reestablishment of civil government, and both President Lincoln and Governor Johnson devoted their efforts to that end. But the Union elements in the state were quarreling among themselves, and new Confederate military attacks were launched. Repeatedly plans had to be postponed. Andrew Johnson, who had not slackened his grueling work pace, was physically exhausted. His wife urged him to take a leave of absence for his health's sake, but he refused. Soldiers did not quit in the middle of a war, he said, and neither would he.

In December 1863, President Lincoln offered an amnesty to all but a handful of Confederates, a plan that included a restoration of citizenship to those who would stop fighting and take an oath of allegiance to the United States Government. Following these guidelines, Johnson ordered that county elections be held in Tennessee in March 1864.

The elections were held, but were a total failure. Union loyalists as well as former Confederates were required to take the oath of allegiance, and many of them felt deeply insulted and refused. Undaunted, Andrew Johnson was determined to try again.

In June 1864 the Republicans held their national convention in Baltimore, renaming themselves the National Union party and calling on all Unionists for support. Governor Johnson sent a delegation from Tennessee, and its only instructions embodied the core of his convictions: They were to sponsor a resolution to the effect that the state's secession had been illegal, as there were no provisions for such a move under the Constitution. Consequently Tennessee had never left the Union.

The delegation, on its own initiative, endorsed President Lincoln for nomination and gave unanimous support to Governor Johnson as a "favorite son" candidate for Vice President. Johnson himself had no part in the making of this decision and did not take it seriously. In fact, a letter he wrote to his son-in-law, Judge Patterson, indicated his hope that he would return to Washington as one of Tennessee's senators. Of all the many public offices he had held in his lifetime, he enjoyed that of United States Senator more than any other.

President Lincoln had other ideas. In order to broaden the party's appeal he wanted a Democrat of demonstrated loyalty as his running mate. His first choice was the controversial and eccentric General Ben

Butler of Massachusetts, currently on military duty. But Butler wasn't interested, in part because he was eager to win fresh military laurels and, equally important, because he privately thought the President could not be reelected.

Lincoln promptly chose Andrew Johnson, a man of unquestioned loyalty to the Union and one who had achieved popularity throughout the entire North.

The convention accepted the President's choice without a murmur.

3

Andrew Johnson accepted the nomination for the Vice Presidency of the United States as a wartime obligation and was neither flattered nor particularly pleased. In a brief acceptance statement, he emphasized the need for unity to win the war and a concerted movement thereafter to restore the whole nation.

For the present he was far more concerned about the renewed Confederate efforts to retake Tennessee, and he worked closely with the Federal commander, General George Thomas. The President's amnesty program, which was being tried out in Tennessee, was not successful, and Johnson was overwhelmed by problems of day-to-day administration.

Lincoln and his followers were worried about the political threat mounted by his Democratic opponent, former General George B. McClellan. Therefore, Johnson, who was known as an effective orator, was swamped with speaking requests from other states. He was forced to decline almost all of them on the grounds that his duties kept him in Tennessee, and even there he spent little time campaigning. He did manage to make one trip to Indiana, where he delivered a number of addresses before large, enthusiastic audiences.

The election was held on November 8, 1864, and the

electoral vote of 212 for Lincoln and only 21 for McClellan did not accurately reflect public feeling. Out of 4 million votes cast, the President won a popular majority of only 400,000.

Andrew Johnson was now Vice-President-elect of the United States. He had little chance to rejoice, however. Confederate General John Bell Hood, defeated by General William T. Sherman at Atlanta, decided to try taking Tennessee, thereby diverting Sherman from his goal of marching up the eastern seaboard. To prevent this, General Thomas distracted Hood, drawing him deep into Tennessee. The Battle of Nashville, fought December 15–16, 1864, was the climax of the campaign. There, Thomas won one of the most decisive victories of the entire war, smashing Hood's army and sending the few survivors fleeing into Alabama. For the first time since the outbreak of the war, Tennessee was permanently secure in Union hands.

Before leaving for Washington, Johnson wanted to see a new civil government installed in Tennessee, and in February a plebiscite was held, annulling the ordinance of secession and acts passed by the Rebel legislature, ending slavery in the state for all time, and electing a new legislature. An exhausted Andrew Johnson had completed his work as military governor. A new governor was elected, "Parson" William G. Brownlow.

Johnson was suffering from a severe attack of malaria. He resigned his office, arose prematurely from his sickbed, and left Nashville late in February. He arrived in Washington on March 1 and occupied the same tiny boardinghouse suite in which he had lived as a senator. But he was too ill to see the many office seekers and other politicians who clamored for his attention, and went straight to bed. There he remained until March 4, the day of the Inauguration, Lincoln's second, his first. He was not even well enough to attend a modest reception at the White House on the evening of March 3.

On the morning of March 4 he was escorted to the Senate, where he was scheduled to take the oath of office, and while awaiting the appointed hour he rested in the Vice President's private quarters. He was still ill and felt so wretched that, shortly before going into the Senate chamber, he accepted a drink of whiskey from his predecessor, outgoing Vice President Hannibal Hamlin of Maine. Johnson took a stiff drink.

Never a teetotaler, Andrew Johnson was nevertheless abstemious and took a drink only rarely. No one had ever seen him intoxicated either in public or in private. On this occasion, however, he was still suffering from malaria, and he had eaten little or nothing for days. The liquor went to his head.

Walking down the center aisle of the Senate chamber, he stumbled twice and was forced to lean on Hamlin's arm. After taking the oath of office, he was expected to make an address of no more than five minutes' duration. Instead he made a rambling speech that lasted for almost twenty minutes, and frequently slurred his words. Many of his listeners were outraged, and he instantly acquired a reputation as a drunkard. The accusation was false and unfair, but in the years that followed, his enemies gave him no opportunity to forget the unfortunate occasion.

The new Vice President recovered sufficiently to listen to Abraham Lincoln's justly renowned Second Inaugural Address. The President summarized his humane policy of reconciliation in words that continue to live:

With malice toward none; with charity for all; with firmness in the right, as God gives us to see the right, let us strive to finish the work we are in; to bind up the nation's wounds; to care for him who shall have borne the battle, and for his widow and his orphan—to do all which may achieve and cherish a just and lasting peace among ourselves and with all nations.

The radicals, led by Sumner and Wade, Thaddeus Stevens, and Ben Butler, were determined to pursue a vindictive policy against the South when the war ended in what was now inevitably regarded as a victory for the Union. States that had seceded would be severely punished and reduced to the level of colonies. Former slaves would take the power and prerogatives of those who had been their masters.

President Lincoln's one desire, as enunciated in his Second Inaugural Address, was to reconcile and reunite the two sections of the country, end discord, and build a true peace in which North and South worked together, putting the horrors of the Civil War behind them.

Vice President Johnson totally and emphatically agreed with him. He, too, wanted the Union restored under the Constitution. He and his family had suffered badly during the war. Mrs. Johnson's health was precarious, he was exhausted, and their property in Greeneville, battered and misused, was just in the process of being restored to them. They had lost a son and a son-in-law, and their second son, Colonel Robert Johnson, was showing the effects of his military service by behaving unpredictably and sometimes drinking to excess.

Yet Andrew Johnson, in his chief's words, felt malice toward none and charity for all. The coming of peace would give the United States the opportunity, at long last, to accomplish the goals in which he had always believed. The people of America, of states north and south, would band together in one Union and obey the law of the land as enunciated in the Constitution.

In spite of the scandal Johnson created, the President supported him unequivocally, telling visitors he was no drunkard. Others who knew him even better than Lincoln said the same thing. Had an assassin's bullet not propelled him into even greater prominence, this minor incident in Andrew Johnson's life would soon have been forgotten.

The Vice President now assumed his Constitutional responsibility, that of presiding over the Senate.

On April 2, 1865, General Lee was compelled to evacuate Richmond, the Confederate capital, and the following day it was occupied by Federal troops. The end at last was within sight. A week later General Lee surrendered to General Grant at Appomattox Court House. The radicals were now afraid that Lincoln's peace terms would be too lenient.

On the night of April 14, President Lincoln finally relaxed for an evening by attending a performance of a play at Ford's Theater called *Our American Cousin*. Vice President Johnson was invited to attend, too, but declined. He was unfamiliar with theaters and knew he wouldn't feel comfortable. Besides, he was still recuperating from his illness, so he intended to read for a short time and then retire.

He was awakened late in the evening by friends, who brought him news of a nightmare: President Lincoln had been shot by a demented actor, John Wilkes Booth, in what was obviously a concerted attack by a band of

fanatics. Secretary of State Seward, too, had been attacked and severely wounded, and an assault on Johnson
had also been planned but had miscarried. The friends
formed a bodyguard around the Vice President.

At 2 A.M. on the morning of April 15, Vice President
Johnson, accompanied by a small military escort, went
to the house opposite Ford's Theater to which Lincoln
had been carried, and spent a few moments looking
down at the dying President. His manner grave, he
returned to his lodgings and there, with several friends
in attendance, spent the rest of the night pacing up and
down.

At 7:30 A.M. Major General Henry W. Halleck, whom
he had known in Tennessee, arrived to inform him that
under no circumstances should he leave his quarters
without an appropriate bodyguard. General Halleck was
so overcome by emotion that he offered no explanation,
but none was needed. Church bells began to toll slowly,
and Andrew Johnson knew that the great Illinoisan was
dead.

At 8 A.M. Secretary of the Treasury Hugh McCulloch
and Attorney General James Speed arrived as official
emissaries of the Cabinet to inform Johnson of what had
happened. They were followed by Chief Justice Salmon
P. Chase, who offered to administer the oath as soon as
he had checked into the legalities.

When the Chief Justice returned at 10 A.M. a small
group awaited him in the parlor of the lodging house. A
pale, shaken Andrew Johnson was sworn in as
seventeenth President of the United States.

He spoke only a few words, then asked the members
of the Cabinet who were present to stay behind, and
requested them to remain in office. Accompanying them

to the Treasury, he met with the entire Cabinet, the wounded Secretary Seward excepted, and repeated his request. His dignity made a deep impression on the group.

He sent a telegram to Eliza, telling her he was safe and had just taken the oath of office as President. She and Martha replied in telegrams assuring him they were offering prayers for him. A few days later he received warm letters from his wife and both of his daughters. He had no time to write in return, but in a telegram he suggested that they wait until Mrs. Lincoln vacated the White House, at which time he would send for them.

Services for President Lincoln were held at the White House on April 19, and marked the first time President Johnson had entered the place since his elevation. On April 21 another service was held at the Capitol, which the new President also attended, and Abraham Lincoln's body was placed on board a funeral train that would carry him to Illinois for burial.

The radicals regarded Lincoln's death as an opportunity to crack down hard on the South, and a number spoke hysterically of hanging Jefferson Davis and other Confederate leaders. Senator Sumner ignored the protocol that prohibited him from calling on the new President until his presence was requested. He paid an unannounced visit to the modest lodging house, and delivered to Johnson a long harangue in which he advised that severe measures be taken against the South. President Johnson listened courteously, but made no reply.

None of the complicated matters that occupied various government departments and bureaus was familiar to Andrew Johnson, and he knew equally little about much of the proposed legislation being drawn up in various Congressional committees. So he took what was in effect a concentrated course of study, holding daily meetings with the Cabinet, individual sessions with its various members, and other meetings with leaders of the Senate and House. He spent so many hours each day reading documents that his eyes watered incessantly, and he grew so tired of sitting that he had a special desk made for him that could be used while standing up.

Establishing temporary quarters at the Treasury in a room adjoining Secretary McCulloch's office, President Johnson worked from 7 A.M. until 1 or 2 the following morning. His lunch consisted of crackers and tea. He completely forgot dinner until someone brought him a meal, and then he was too preoccupied and tired to eat. At no time, McCulloch noted, did he touch whiskey.

Colonel Robert Johnson appeared unbidden and unannounced in Washington, and Secretary of War Stanton, not bothering to consult the President, officially gave him an appointment as a military aide-de-camp to his father. The President disliked nepotism, but the appointment had been made, and he quickly discovered that a close relative could perform tasks for him that were beyond the scope of outsiders.

Robert made himself very useful, going on confidential errands and trying to shield his father from the hordes who sought the ear of the President. He also tried to persuade him to eat more substantial meals and to spend more than three or four hours in bed each night, but these efforts were in vain. The President maintained a schedule even more blistering than that which had caused his family concern when he had been military governor of Tennessee.

Now many people were worried about him. He

traveled between his lodging house and his temporary office in a carriage, took no exercise, and worked incessantly, reading and conferring, trying to master the intricacies of government in a short time. He had not recovered completely from his bout of malaria, and his health remained precarious. His back ached so constantly that he used his stand-up desk exclusively. He also walked with a slight limp, and used a gold-headed cane that Robert had purchased on his behalf. Secretary Stanton and Secretary of the Navy Gideon Welles, upon whom Lincoln had relied and who would become Johnson's faithful friend, were afraid he would soon collapse.

If anything untoward happened to Johnson, Ben Wade, the president pro tempore of the Senate, would succeed him. Senator Wade was such an opinionated bigot that reasonable men shuddered at the thought.

The radicals, who commanded overwhelming majorities in both the Senate and the House, had been opposed from the outset to President Lincoln's policy of reconciliation, under which the full rights of the Southern states were to be restored as rapidly and judiciously as possible. This had been Lincoln's aim in Tennessee, where the experiment had first been made, and Governor Johnson had been his enthusiastic collaborator.

But the radicals assumed that President Johnson shared their vindictive point of view, totally ignoring or overlooking the many statements on the subject he had made in Nashville. Because he was himself a Southerner who had suffered at the hands of the Confederacy, they took it for granted that he would stand with them. They were completely mistaken.

Johnson was determined that Jefferson Davis and a

handful of other Confederate leaders be punished, and was equally firm in his demand that President Lincoln's assassin and others who had taken part in the conspiracy be brought to justice. But he was also insistent that the rights of full citizenship be given back to all but a few Southerners, and that their state governments begin to function as soon as possible.

In the emotional atmosphere that gripped the North at the end of the war, not many shared the new President's view. One of the few who did was General Sherman, the second-ranking Federal commander after Grant. Ironically, he was a brother of Senator John Sherman of Ohio, one of the radical leaders.

Late in April a half dozen suspects in the plot against President Lincoln and his principal aides were taken into custody, and Booth, who had assassinated the President, was killed in Virginia. Secretary of War Stanton, who might well have been called emotionally unbalanced had he lived a hundred years later, was convinced that Jefferson Davis was personally responsible for the conspiracy. He offered no concrete evidence for this belief, which is not surprising, for the charge was false. But he soon had the whole North clamoring for Davis' hanging. When Davis was caught on May 10, he promptly branded the charge ridiculous, and many Northerners who had known him as a senator prior to the war agreed that he was no murderer. Nevertheless, the mere fact that such an accusation could be made in all seriousness by a high-ranking Cabinet member is indicative of the hysteria of the times.

Late in May a victory parade was held in Washington, and various members of the Senate and House were present on the reviewing stand with President Johnson.

It was one of the last occasions their relations would be cordial.

The President issued two proclamations serving notice on the radicals that he had his own ideas on the subject of the Reconstruction of the Union and intended to follow them. In one he offered an amnesty to most who had taken part in the rebellion. In the second he established a step-by-step plan that would lead to a return to full statehood for North Carolina. Similar proclamations soon followed for each of the other former Confederate states.

He made it plain that he intended to restore the Union intact, as it had been prior to the war. The one exception to this status was that slavery was abolished for all time in the United States.

This stand immediately brought him into direct conflict with such congressmen as Pennsylvania's Thaddeus Stevens, who invariably referred to the South as "conquered territory." The political battle was joined by the summer of 1865. President Johnson appointed provisional governors for each of the Southern states, but the radicals refused to recognize them. His son-in-law, Judge Patterson, was elected to the Senate from Tennessee, but the Congress refused to seat any member of that state's delegation. The President had been careful to insist that, as a requisite for recognition, each of the Southern states ratify the Thirteenth Amendment to the Constitution, which abolished slavery, but this was insufficient for either the Senate or the House. They and the new President were on a collision course.

At the beginning of the summer, Eliza Johnson arrived in Washington with her youngest son, her daughters, and her five grandchildren. They soon took up residence in the White House, and the precarious state of Mrs. Johnson's health, which confined her to the family quarters most of the time, made it necessary for Martha Patterson to act as her father's official hostess. She also took charge of refurnishing and cleaning the White House, which had become shabby during the war years.

The change in President Johnson's disposition became evident almost as soon as his family joined him. His wife's presence calmed him and made him less abrasive. Each afternoon he went out for a carriage ride, accompanied by his grandchildren, and while they scrambled about on the banks of the Potomac River, he threw stones into the water. Mrs. Patterson soon inaugurated a series of official dinners and receptions, and Andrew Johnson looked years younger. His back bothered him less frequently, and although he continued to walk with the aid of his cane, his limp was no longer pronounced.

At no time did he or any member of his family put on airs. On one occasion Mrs. Johnson is supposed to have said, "We're plain people from Tennessee, and after we've spent our required time here, we're going straight home to our own kind of living." The remark has also been attributed to Mrs. Patterson, and whether she said it or her mother, the sentiment is the same, and the whole family shared it.

In July the President signed an order confirming the death sentence for the conspirators who had taken part in the plot against President Lincoln and his cabinet. Four persons were hanged, among them Mrs. Mary Surratt, a Washington boardinghouse keeper whose guilt was somewhat in doubt. The President did not know, until the time of his own impeachment, when he was severely criticized for not having shown clemency to Mrs. Surratt, that a pardon had been prepared for his signature. It had been deliberately withheld by Secretary Stanton.

The chorus of Congressional opposition to the President's overall program of restoring the Southern states to their former place in the Union became increasingly loud through the summer of 1865. Ben Wade spoke for all of the radicals when he declared, "We have in truth already lost the whole moral effect of our victories over the rebellion. The golden opportunity for humiliating and destroying the influence of the Southern aristocracy has gone forever."

What neither he nor his like-minded Northern colleagues could understand was that President Johnson was not trying to restore the aristocrats of the South to their former place of power and wealth. It was ironic in the extreme that such a charge should be made against him. He was a member of the poor-white class, which the aristocratic Southern planters despised. Not only did he still regard himself as a member of that class, but it was in their interest that he was pressing the cause of reconciliation. What the radicals didn't realize, but the President well knew, was that the Southern planters continued to look down their noses at Johnson and thought of him as a social inferior. But these subtleties were beyond the grasp of men like Sumner, Wade, and Stevens, who demanded the abasement of the entire South.

The President was convinced his own course was right, and pushed ahead, encouraged by reports from the South that progress was both rapid and solid. The fact that the Congress was in recess during the late summer and autumn made his task easier.

When the Thirty-Ninth Congress convened early in December 1865, a clash with the President was inevitable. Andrew Johnson would be required to pay the penalty for the power his predecessor had exerted. Abraham Lincoln had been an exceptionally strong Chief Executive, his position enhanced by the fact that the nation had been at war, and members of both the Senate and House were determined to reassert their own control.

Their worst mistake, perhaps, was their inability to judge the character of President Johnson. Many had served with him in one or both houses, and they thought they knew him as a genial politician preoccupied with land grants and similar questions. Although his record should have spoken for itself, few of his former colleagues recognized the depth of his devotion to the Constitution.

His own greatest error, perhaps, was his failure to articulate his position. His dedication to the Union, under the Constitution, was so great that he may have felt it unnecessary to spell out his stand. Whatever the reasons, the Congress believed he would ride with a new tide, while he thought that the Senate and House would respect the Constitutional balance of powers. He was willing to give the legislative branch its due, and assumed that congressmen and senators would be equally courteous in their treatment of the executive branch.

The case of Alexander H. Stephens illustrates the difficulty. A senator from Georgia before the war, he had been one of the few members of the upper chamber to become personally friendly with Andrew Johnson. He had been Vice President of the Confederacy until its collapse, and now his state had returned him to Washington as a senator. As soon as he reached Washington he paid a call on the President, and Johnson, who respected him as a man who had lived according to his convictions, not only bore him no personal animosity but was delighted to greet him as an old friend.

The radicals were outraged. That the President had extended the hospitality of the White House to an arch-villain second only to Jefferson Davis was startling. The mere fact that Johnson had shaken his hand and offered him a glass of sherry was an outrage. The Senate had no intention of seating anyone from Georgia until the state accepted far more stringent regulations than the President had imposed, and under no circumstances would a traitor like Stephens be admitted.

The South, it must be admitted, was doing little to aid its own cause. Stunned by defeat, the politicians of the former Confederacy breathed more easily when they learned of President Johnson's lenient terms for readmission to the Union. Some were still arrogant, others were stupid, and in their greed they pressed too hard and too quickly. Something had to be said for the jaundiced view of the South taken by the radical Republicans at a time when the wounds of war were not yet healed.

One Southern state after another adopted "black codes" that, in effect, would have perpetuated slavery. Ordered to repudiate their Confederate war debts, one Southern state after another procrastinated. These and similar actions fed the suspicions of the radicals, who were convinced that the South, after losing the war, intended to cheat and lie in an attempt to win the peace.

Andrew Johnson, like Abraham Lincoln before him, sought only a reunited nation, and was caught in the middle.

The problems of peace were overwhelming. How was the newly freed black man going to earn a living? How soon, under the pending Fourteenth Amendment, would the former slave be granted the right to vote? Equally important, how would illiterate men be prepared for citizenship? Other problems were staggering, too. The radicals might make pious declarations in support of blacks, but their own Northern states were guilty of racial discrimination, too. The South was still in an economic shambles, with agricultural production hampered and seaports closed. Hundreds of thousands of Confederate military veterans had to be given opportunities to earn a living. Efforts had to be made to build new industries in the crippled South, and the disrupting influence of carpetbaggers—Northerners seeking their own advancement at the expense of the defeated Confederacy—had to be restricted.

Even if the President and the Congress had been able to work together in harmony, the task of Reconstruction would have been enormous. With the White House pulling in one direction and Capitol Hill in another, the struggle became doubly difficult.

Congressman Thaddeus Stevens had made up his mind that Congress alone would determine the nature and terms of Reconstruction. He made his views plain in a private talk with President Johnson immediately prior to the opening of the Congress. Senators Sumner and Wade felt the same way and were equally candid.

Andrew Johnson, whose lack of subtlety was one of his

greatest handicaps, was blunt, too. The Constitution granted certain powers to the Executive, and he was determined to exercise them to the best of his ability. Neither cajolery nor threats moved him.

The Congress moved first, forming a Joint Committee on Reconstruction under the chairmanship of Stevens.

The President failed to realize how far his opponents were prepared to go in their efforts to take the helm. The men sent to Washington by Tennessee had been loyal to the Union throughout the war, and had suffered personal hardships, including imprisonment, for their beliefs. Therefore, he reasoned, it was inconceivable that they would be rejected. The radicals in the House and Senate flexed their muscles, and refused to seat the Tennessee delegation. In the process this insulted the President himself. The issue was joined.

The President countered with his first State of the Union message, delivered to the Congress immediately thereafter. Under no circumstances, he declared, would he allow the South to be ruled by force as a conquered territory. It was imperative that the nation be reunited and that the states of the former Confederacy be permitted to reassume their constitutional functions.

The newspapers of the North applauded the statesmanlike message, and the press of Great Britain and the principal nations of Europe echoed them. The radical Republicans said little and bided their time. They had the votes to impose their will on the President and the nation, and they had no intention of engaging in a debate about principles. Only results mattered.

Although President Johnson did not realize it at the time, he did not command the full support of his Cabinet.

Navy Secretary Welles was unswervingly loyal to him, and so was Treasury Secretary McCulloch. Secretary of State Seward, who was sufficiently recovered from the attempt on his life to return to work during the summer of 1865, gradually came to appreciate Andrew Johnson's strengths and not only supported him but became one of his canniest advisers.

War Secretary Stanton was the troublemaker. Emotionally unstable and harboring secret hopes that he might some day become President himself, he pretended he was acting in good faith in his dealings with Andrew Johnson. In reality, however, he maintained secret relations with the radical leaders, and privately kept them informed of strategies determined at Cabinet meetings.

Ultimately Stanton's colleagues began to suspect he was not to be trusted, and warned the President. But Andrew Johnson hesitated. Even when Stanton's disloyalty became obvious and could no longer be doubted, he put off taking action. Not until it was too late did Johnson discharge his Secretary of War. Of all the mistakes he made in the events that led to his impeachment, his failure to take vigorous steps to rid his Cabinet of Stanton may have been his worst weakness. He was trying to maintain some semblance of harmony within the ranks of his official family, it is true, but no historian has been able to explain why this ordinarily forthright, decisive man harmed himself and the cause to which he was devoted by being so dilatory.

Attorney General Speed tried to play both the President's game and that of the Congress, as did Secretary of the Interior James Harlan. Johnson was quick to realize what they were doing, stopped confiding in them, and eventually got rid of them. But he clung to Stanton, perhaps because the Secretary of War had supported him when he had been military governor of Tennessee. It is difficult to find any other reason.

The President was deficient, too, in his handling of pardon seekers. Southerners by the thousands overran the White House. Few were turned away, and thousands received presidential pardons. Even moderate Northerners were disturbed, and Northern newspapers became critical of what they called the "spectacle" of a Southern President "entertaining" the nation's former foes at the Executive Mansion. Years would pass before the nation would realize that Andrew Johnson, always true to himself, was consistently practicing the tolerance he preached.

In his earnest desire to be fair to the defeated section of the country and his deep desire to see the nation reunited under the Constitution, he appears to have been unaware of a basic fact of life recognized by most Americans who held high office: The defeated South still hated the victorious North.

To an extent the problem was unavoidable. In Andrew Johnson's day, as in later times, the President was isolated, which made it difficult for him to glean the true facts of any situation. Pardon seekers took care to conceal their real feelings from him, which compounded the difficulty.

Many Northerners agreed with the President that the nation should put the past aside and rebuild. But the South refused to forget the war and could not forget its consequences. So the intransigence of the people President Johnson was trying to help, thanks to his lofty ideals and uncompromising principles, actually harmed him as well as their own cause.

A tragedy unique in American history was in the making.

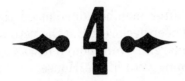

President Johnson's lenient Reconstruction policy, Senator Sumner said, was "the greatest mistake which history ever recorded. The President is worse than Jeff Davis—the evil he has inflicted on the country is incalculable."

That comment was one of the kindest made about Andrew Johnson by the radicals in 1866. Others were already saying he was an obstacle in the path of Reconstruction and would have to be removed.

The first crisis of the year occurred on February 10. The Congress had passed a new Freedmen's Bureau Bill, which not only offered increased help and protection to former slaves, but so severely penalized those who had been their masters that the economic suffering of the South would be prolonged for years.

President Johnson vetoed the bill on the ground that it unnecessarily increased the military powers of the Federal government in the South at the expense of civil government, and therefore was unconstitutional.

The bill would revive sectional discords, he declared, and in the long run would do more harm than good. Then, with a remarkable lack of tact, he proceeded to lecture the Senate and House on their duties under the Constitution.

When the veto message was read, the Senate erupted,

and member after member denounced the President. Open war had been declared. But the veto was sustained by a narrow margin, even though it was overridden by an overwhelming vote in the House.

President Johnson was stung by these personal attacks of senators. A few evenings later, when a friendly crowd marched to the White House and called for a speech, he forgot presidential dignity. He had spent his entire political life in Tennessee, where stump oratory demanded that attacks be answered in kind, so he responded with a vigorous, Tennessee-style address in which he not only counterattacked but indulged in the same name-calling his opponents had used.

The crowd loved the speech, but in print it was vulgar and unseemly. Even the moderate press was shocked, and Secretaries Welles and McCulloch begged the President not to make any more impromptu addresses. The delighted radicals kept the issue alive by making fresh assaults on a man they pictured as an inept bumbler.

The President rejected all criticism of his talk. He had been on the receiving end of attacks for a long time, and it was not his nature to remain passive. He had drawn blood. He felt he had accomplished something in placing his views before the public, and he was determined to strike again when the opportunity arose.

In March a so-called Civil Rights Bill was sent to the White House, and the President vetoed it. Not only was it unconstitutional, but it was also inconsistent, because it discriminated against blacks in the North whereas it protected those in the South.

In a close vote, the Senate overrode the veto, but in the House the anti-Johnson margin far exceeded the two thirds necessary. Thaddeus Stevens indicated the true aim of the radicals when he told the House, "Andrew Johnson must learn that he is your servant, and that as Congress shall order he must obey. There is no escape from it. God forbid that he should have one title of power except what he derives through Congress and the Constitution. . . . He and his minions must learn that this is not a government of kings and satraps, but a government of the people, and that Congress is the people."

Some well-informed men saw handwriting scrawled in large letters on the wall. General Sherman, stationed at U.S. Army headquarters in St. Louis, wrote a personal letter to the President in which he said that "the extreme radical measures of Sumner & Stevens were calculated to lead to a result that even they ought not to desire, viz., the everlasting estrangement of all the people of the South."

The fundamental issue at stake became clear to Andrew Johnson: The Congress was trying to strip the President of his powers under the Constitution. He could point, with accuracy, to speech after speech in both the Senate and the House that clearly indicated this was the undoubted goal of the radicals. He would oppose them, he said, by every means possible.

Late in the spring of 1866, the Tennessee delegation to the Congress was at long last seated. But the feelings against the President were so strong that one member was temporarily excluded: Senator-elect Patterson would not be admitted until a special committee investigated his loyalty.

The very idea of such an inquiry was absurd. Patterson had spent more than two years in Confederate prisons because he had refused to abandon his faith in the Union. Even after his release, he and his family had been subjected to constant harassment and insults, and the windows of his house had been broken so many times by hoodlums that he had finally boarded them up until the end of the war.

A number of moderate Republican newspapers lost no time saying that it was ridiculous to investigate a man of Patterson's standing. But the radicals ignored these comments. They were riding high, and their campaign against Andrew Johnson was just beginning to gain momentum.

The attacks on the President continued unabated in the summer, after the Congress adjourned. Again Andrew Johnson counterattacked by calling for a convention to meet in Philadelphia, in August, for the purpose of promoting support for pro-Johnson candidates in the forthcoming Congressional elections.

The convention was doomed from the outset by bad planning and a lack of sufficient time. On July 30 a vicious race riot erupted in New Orleans, giving the radical press the opportunity to claim that white brutality was still rampant in the South. Thaddeus Stevens took advantage of the situation to make the preposterous claim that Andrew Johnson was personally responsible for the riot. Senator Sumner picked up the cry.

The President, stunned by the riot, immediately ordered the Army to restore order. Then he learned that Stanton could have prevented the riot if he had acted decisively on information he had previously received. He was coldly furious with the Secretary of War, who made excuses for himself while confiding to friends that he shared the belief that the President had been responsible for the bloodshed.

The National Union convention was held in Philadelphia in mid-August, with all states represented, including those whose governments had not yet been sanctioned by the Congress. On the surface it was highly successful, and President Johnson was encouraged. But neither he nor his supporters took into account political realities. The convention was attended by moderates of every persuasion, but they were in a distinct minority.

The mood in the North favored the radical Republicans, whereas most Democrats, struggling to regain their own identity, had no desire to be submerged beneath a National Union blanket. The more aggressive politicians in the South also leaned toward their traditional, prewar Democratic affiliation.

The President's supporters, therefore, were men of goodwill who lacked power bases of their own. They shared Andrew Johnson's concept of reconciliation, and because they felt as he did, Johnson allowed himself to be deceived, thinking that his policy had a true national appeal.

How this could have happened is not difficult to understand. With the exception of the 1864 election, when he had campaigned only in his own state and Indiana and had been elected as Vice President because he had been Lincoln's running mate, he had spent all of his long political career only in Tennessee, where he had been elected to virtually every office available.

But he had no real idea of what voters in New England, the mid-Atlantic states, the Middle West, or the Far West favored. He was not in direct contact with them, and learned about them only from men who felt as he did. Consequently he was misled.

The seeming success of the National Union convention

gave the President an idea: He would take his case directly to the people of the United States, in what he called a "swing round the circle." Late in August, he left Washington on board a special train that would carry him into ten states in a journey that would last three weeks.

The "swing round the circle" was ill conceived, badly planned, and poorly executed. The results were catastrophic. Radical Republican governors, mayors, senators, and congressmen were conspicuous by their absence, and most of the crowds who showed up to hear the President were radicals, who were hostile to him. The radical Republican press saw an opportunity to ridicule him and presented him at a disadvantage.

President Johnson failed to realize that a national tour in no way resembled a speaking trip in Tennessee. Throughout his career he had grown accustomed to making the same address at every stop, and this had been effective in Knoxville, Chattanooga, Nashville, and Memphis. On this journey, however, he was accompanied by reporters who gave him national coverage, and who became bored when he delivered almost identical talks in New York, Pittsburgh, and Chicago.

Andrew Johnson created additional problems for himself by reverting to old habits. When he was heckled—as he frequently was—he replied to his tormentors in his best rough-and-tumble Tennessee stump-speaking style. This technique had been effective in frontier Nashville and river-port Memphis, but it shocked his audiences in the sophisticated cities of the North.

The radicals were quick to take advantage of the lack of dignity he displayed and began to insinuate that he was drunk. These stories were complete fabrications, but strong hints to the effect that he was intoxicated appeared in a number of radical newspapers. As a matter of fact, the only member of the President's party who really drank to excess was General Grant, but he was the most popular of Northern heroes, and not one word about his lack of discretion appeared in print.

The President was surrounded by a prestigious group that included Secretary of State Seward and Secretary of the Navy Welles. Admiral David G. Farragut, the Navy's great hero, also accompanied the President, and in addition to Grant seven other generals were in the party. There were a number of ladies in the group, too, among them Martha Patterson, Mrs. Farragut, and Mrs. Welles.

The President opened the tour in Philadelphia with a plea for national unity, and his words were received politely, but without enthusiasm. Then he was cheered in New York, and the radicals went to work in earnest, deliberately packing his audiences with radical sympathizers.

Applause grew sparse as the tour moved westward through the state of New York, and the President began to press harder, his manner becoming more aggressive. Then the heckling began, and Johnson replied in kind, his attitude often harshly abrasive. In Buffalo the President was tired. In Cleveland he lost his temper. In Detroit he was greeted by lukewarm audiences. In Chicago he had to make his way through lines of anti-Johnson pickets. In St. Louis he lost his temper again. In Indianapolis an anti-Johnson riot broke out. Louisville cheered the President in the most generous reception he had received to date, but he was booed in Pittsburgh. And in scores of smaller communities, where he made whistle-stop speeches, people were either apathetic or hostile.

Newspapers that had been supporting President Johnson began to edge away from him. Politicians who had been following him realized he had little popular support throughout the North and turned away from him. The net result of his trip was a strengthening of the radical Republicans in every state he had visited. Not even Sumner, Wade, and Stevens could have achieved better results if they had planned his junket themselves. The stump-speaking style that Tennessee loved was anathema to crowds in the North, and the trip was a complete failure.

Congressional and local elections took place in several states in October, with the balance held in November, and everywhere the results were the same. The radical Republicans had triumphed, and in both the State and the House of Representatives they would command far more than the two-thirds majority necessary to override a presidential veto.

President Johnson was "a dead horse," Thaddeus Stevens said, and suggested it might be a good idea to get rid of him. Ben Wade, as President pro tempore of the Senate, would move into the White House, and the radicals would have clear sailing.

Secretary of War Stanton, who had been walking a political tightrope for many months, secretly cast his lot with the radicals. At the same time he continued to pretend, both in private conversations with the President and at Cabinet meetings, that his loyalty to Johnson was unwavering.

The new Congress, which included Ben Butler as a member of the House, convened on December 3, 1866.

The President's State of the Union message was received in silence, and, as one commentator observed, "Congress wanted the President's head on a platter."

Senator Sumner immediately introduced a bill granting the franchise to blacks in the District of Columbia. The radicals pushed through the measure without trouble, even though, as several Cabinet members observed, they lacked the integrity to grant the vote to blacks in their home states.

On January 4, 1867, President Johnson vetoed the bill, as anticipated, and it was passed over his veto by overwhelming votes.

On January 7 Representative James M. Ashley of Ohio introduced a resolution: "I do impeach Andrew Johnson, Vice President and acting President of the United States, of high crimes and misdemeanors." The resolution instructed the Committee on the Judiciary to investigate his conduct in office to determine whether he "has been guilty of acts which are designated or calculated to overthrow, subvert or corrupt the government of the United States."

The resolution was passed by a vote of 107 to 39. The purpose was so obviously political, with no basis in fact, that 45 Republicans abstained, even though Thaddeus Stevens threatened all Republicans who failed to follow the party line with a loss of patronage and influence.

President Johnson ignored the resolution, and instead concentrated his attention on the proposed new Military Reconstruction Bill, a harsh measure, introduced in the House by Stevens, that would treat the South like a conquered territory. At a Cabinet meeting on January 8, Secretary Seward expressed the firm opinion that no sovereign state could be reduced to the status of a con-

79

quered land. The other members agreed, with only Secretary Stanton qualifying his position with so many contradictory remarks that no one knew where he stood.

The radicals rammed the bill through both the House and the Senate.

Even more damaging to the President's cause was another measure, the Tenure of Office Act. This bill provided that no Federal officeholder whose presidential appointment had been confirmed by the Senate could be removed by the President unless the Senate concurred. As a small sop to the presidential power and dignity, the bill did permit the President to suspend an officeholder in the event the Congress was not in session.

Cabinet members, under the terms of this measure, would "hold their office respectively for and during the term of the President by whom they may have been appointed, and for one month thereafter, subject to removal by and with the consent of the Senate." Secretaries Seward, Welles, and Stanton had been appointed by President Lincoln, and consequently were offered no protection.

A number of radicals in both the Senate and House called this omission to the attention of their colleagues. But the majority, although opposed to President Johnson, were honorable men who were sincere in their beliefs, and were reluctant to include an amendment that would further shackle and embarrass the President by making it impossible for him to dismiss these three Cabinet members if he wanted to be rid of them. In its final form the bill continued to offer them no protection.

The humiliating Tenure of Office Act was duly passed by both the House and the Senate and, along with the

Military Reconstruction Bill, was sent to the White House.

The President consulted at length with his Cabinet, and on March 2, 1867, the last day of the congressional session, he vetoed both bills on the ground that they were unconstitutional. Both were passed over his veto before the Senate and House adjourned.

Many serious-minded men throughout the country were alarmed by the hatred of the radicals for the President and by their vindictiveness toward the South. General Sherman summarized this concern in a letter to his brother, in which he said, "If the President is impeached and the South reduced to territories, the country will, of course, relapse into a state of war, or quasi-war, and what good it will do passes my comprehension."

The Fortieth Congress convened on March 4, two days after its predecessor's term expired. So far the Committee on the Judiciary had been unable to find any evidence on which to impeach the President, so it opened an investigation of his personal finances. He could have balked, but cooperated willingly, and the embarrassed congressmen learned that instead of investing in various corporations, as they had hoped, he had placed every penny he had ever saved in United States Government bonds. They were unable to claim he had taken advantage of his high office for personal gain; on the contrary, he had demonstrated his faith in the long-range future of his country. That phase of the congressional investigation was dropped, and the radicals did not mention it again.

Instead they launched a campaign to isolate him, and concentrated their attention on General Grant, perhaps the most popular man in the country. The head of the Army had remained loyal to his Commander-in-Chief, but he was ambitious, and the radicals painted a glowing portrait of the future in store for him. Grant was a sincere man of limited intellect, and the radicals knew they could handle him, so they had decided he would be the perfect candidate for President in 1868. The general was flattered, and because he was dealing with sophisticated, clever men, he had no idea that he was being wooed, much less won.

Grant edged into the radical camp without realizing it. At no time did he consciously or deliberately disobey a presidential order, which would have been contrary to his nature. But his cooperation with President Johnson became half-hearted, and inasmuch as he reported to the White House through Secretary Stanton, who was in no hurry to obey presidential directives, he was in a position to do as he pleased.

There was a flurry of excitement in May, when the President signed an order transferring Jefferson Davis from military custody to that of the civil courts, where he would stand trial for treason. Secretary Stanton violently opposed the transfer. The President privately agreed with him, but felt the law was clear on the subject and that he had no choice.

Davis was set free on bail, and for a short time the radicals believed they had a new club with which to belabor the President. Then they discovered that Andrew Johnson believed Davis should be hanged. Besides that, they knew that under the constitutional separation of powers, the matter had to be decided by the judiciary. So they dropped the idea.

By this time it was becoming clear to the President,

his friends, and his closest associates in the Cabinet that the House of Representatives would manufacture evidence against Johnson if no genuine grounds for removal could be found. On March 30, 1867, Secretary Seward completed negotiations with Imperial Russia for the purchase of the huge territory known as Alaska for a token price of $7.2 million. The Senate grudgingly ratified the treaty of April 9, but gave no credit to either the President or the Secretary of State. In fact, the purchase was ridiculed as "Seward's folly." Nothing done by Andrew Johnson or his Cabinet was deemed worthy of praise.

In the main, Andrew Johnson accepted the attacks of his enemies with good grace. When radicals appeared at White House receptions, he shook hands with them, treated them cordially, and gave no indication he was even aware of their campaign to disgrace him and drive him from office. On occasion, however, his patience wore thin, and when the subject of impeachment was raised at a Cabinet meeting late in the spring of 1867, he growled, "Impeach and be damned!"

By the summer of 1867 there was less talk of impeachment. There were even private indications that a rebellion against the leadership of Sumner in the Senate and Stevens in the House might be brewing. Although the President had vetoed the Military Reconstruction Bill and was opposed to it in principle, it had become law. Even his most dedicated foes were forced to admit he administered the act scrupulously. In fact, a number of radical Republicans who had voted for it saw the problems it created in a hostile South, precisely as the President had feared and predicted.

Some loopholes could be found in the Military Reconstruction Act, and the President took full advantage of them to deal more leniently with the South than the radicals had intended. The Republican press protested, and when the Congress returned to work after the summer recess, the radicals were in a fighting mood. They promptly passed a new Military Reconstruction Act that closed the loopholes. Adding insult to injury, they made General Grant rather than the President responsible for the administration of the new law. The President vetoed the bill, and it was promptly passed over his veto.

Andrew Johnson saw the issues clearly. In their arrogance, the radical Republicans were attempting to destroy the constitutional balance of power by emasculating the executive branch and making it totally subservient to the legislative branch. True to the convictions he had held all his life, he wrote a firm veto message, in which he warned the country of what was happening.

Yet another crisis finally impelled him to get rid of Secretary Stanton. He finally learned that the Secretary of War had deliberately withheld the pardon that would have spared the life of Mary Surratt, and on August 5, 1867, he wrote a short note to the effect that "public considerations of a high character constrain me to say that your resignation as Secretary of War will be accepted."

Stanton delayed for several days. Then he sent a reply in which he declined to resign before Congress returned. Obviously he intended to hide behind the Tenure of Office Act.

On August 11 the President formally suspended Stanton, as he had a right to do under the Tenure of Office Act, and appointed General Grant as acting Secretary.

Stanton no longer had a choice and was forced to vacate his office. Congress had gone off on another recess until November, and in the meantime he was powerless.

General Grant proved to be a poor choice as acting Secretary. His own political ambitions were foremost in his mind, and he balked at carrying out various presidential directives concerning the administration of the South under the Military Reconstruction Act. He replied at length to orders the President gave him, forcing Andrew Johnson to crack down on him repeatedly.

The atmosphere was less than healthy. The Government was breaking down, and the radicals, totally aroused now, were howling for the President's blood.

Elections were held in the autumn of 1867 in many states, and the voters made their opinions very clear. The radical Republicans suffered severe losses, with Democrats and National Union—or Johnson—advocates winning state offices everywhere. Obviously the public throughout the North was rejecting the vindictive policy against the South and approved of President Johnson's policy of reconciliation.

The President remained calm, believing he had been vindicated, but when the radical senators and representatives returned to Washington, they were more determined than ever to get rid of the man in the White House whom they had come to detest. Every time they thought they had smashed him, he stood upright again, displaying remarkable powers of recovery, and they were so incensed they became reckless.

The Congress reconvened on November 21, and it appeared that the Committee on the Judiciary had been unable to find grounds for impeachment. But the radical leadership twisted some arms, and a majority of the committee reported an impeachment bill on November 27.

The measure reached the floor of the House for decision on December 7. The charges against President Johnson were so flimsy and the constitutional grounds on which his position rested were so strong that many radical Republicans, after examining their own consciences, were unable to vote in favor of the bill. The radical leadership found it impossible to obtain the necessary two-thirds majority, and even Thaddeus Stevens was forced to concede that impeachment was no longer possible.

A few days later Secretary of War Stanton returned to Washington from a visit to New England, and his radical Republican friends immediately took up the matter of his suspension from office. The cause of impeachment may have appeared dead, but now it was very much alive again.

5

President Johnson thought he was in an unassailable position, which he explained in detail to his Cabinet. Secretary of War Stanton was not covered by the Tenure of Office Act, and if he wanted to test the constitutionality of his ouster, he would be obliged to bring suit in the Federal courts. The President was eager to see such a test made, believing the courts would sustain him.

The President also reached an understanding with General Grant. In the possible—even probable—event that the Senate restored Stanton to his office, Grant either could keep his post and thus automatically force a court test or, if he decided he didn't want to be placed in the middle of the fight, he could resign as acting Secretary. In the latter event he was to notify the White House in time for the President to appoint a new Secretary, who would refuse to budge and would thus compel the whole issue to be taken to the courts.

Andrew Johnson felt he had been passive long enough. He had been careful to obey the law, including the administration of acts he believed harmful to the future of the country. Now, if the radicals persisted, he was prepared to fight for the Union his enemies were destroying and for the Constitution they were subverting. If they desisted in the wake of their failure to impeach him, all well and good. But if they tried again, he was prepared for battle.

The State of the Union message, which the President sent to the Congress early in December, contained a careful delineation of his principles and his position. Neither the Senate nor the House paid any attention to the message, and adjourned for the Christmas holidays. However, the President and his supporters hoped the country was listening.

On January 10, a Senate committee recommended nonconcurrence in the suspension of Stanton.

On January 11, Grant notified the President of his intention to resign at once as acting Secretary. The following day was a Sunday, and Johnson persuaded him to do nothing until Monday, January 13.

On the thirteenth, the Senate formally voted its non-concurrence and ordered Stanton's reinstatement.

On January 14, General Grant vacated the office of Secretary of War, locking it behind him and handing the key to an aide. Another aide carried his resignation to the White House.

As Grant was leaving the War Department offices, Edwin Stanton arrived and requested that the aide hand him the key. This was done, and he took physical possession of the office of Secretary of War. There he settled down for a siege, visited by victory-claiming senators and congressmen, sleeping on a cot, and eating meals sent in to him by his wife.

The President was furious, and believing that Grant had deliberately betrayed him, he virtually broke personal relations with the general. Certainly Johnson's strategy and tactics were now in complete disarray. He had two problems: how to get rid of Stanton and how to force the court test of the Tenure of Office Act.

Andrew Johnson had been completely denigrated by the radical Republican Congress, with the powers of the Presidency taken from him, and he had been publicly humiliated before the entire country. He had several choices:

1. He could do nothing, remain in the White House as a figurehead and eke out the rest of his term performing meaningless ceremonial functions.

2. He could take his case to the nation, appealing to the people over the heads of senators and congressmen. This course entailed the greatest risks and offered the least hope that he could attain a satisfactory solution.

3. He could strike back at his enemies in a way guaranteed to bring the crisis to a definitive head.

Andrew Johnson never considered any approach but the third. The Constitution was in danger, and the American form of government was on the thin edge of dissolution. Equally important, he was a fighter by nature, and he had been embarrassed enough by men who had pushed him too hard and too far.

Some historians in the latter part of the nineteenth and early portion of the twentieth centuries expressed the opinion that President Johnson chose the wrong issue upon which to make his stand, but the passage of time has placed matters in a different perspective. The various Military Reconstruction acts were complex and difficult for laymen to understand, so the public well might have become confused had the President chosen to make his issue on the grounds that these laws were not constitutional. Republican and Democratic legal experts were divided on various portions of the acts, and it would not have been easy to present a clear picture to the people of the country.

The Tenure of Office case was far different. Even though the act itself was vindictive and probably unconstitutional, it specifically provided Secretary Stanton with no protection. He had been appointed by Lincoln, and consequently was not covered by the provisions of the act.

When Andrew Johnson decided to move, he acted boldly and without hesitation. He summoned his Cabinet and, without asking for advice, informed his immediate subordinates of his intentions.

Secretary Welles expressed the opinion that the House of Representatives had been waiting for just such an opportunity, and undoubtedly would pass an impeachment resolution. The other members of the Cabinet agreed with his analysis.

President Johnson replied calmly that he welcomed such a development. The United States was in jeopardy, he said, and he was prepared to face any consequences in an effort to save the nation.

His strategy was simple. He intended to dismiss Stanton from office, thereby directly challenging the authority of the Congress.

His greatest problem was that of finding someone suitable who was willing to become Secretary of War. His first choice was General Sherman, who refused on the grounds that he would outrank his immediate superior, General Grant. His loyalty to the one general who was senior to him was absolute.

The President spent many days going through lists of potential candidates, and finally decided on a virtual unknown, Major General Lorenzo Thomas. Thomas was adjutant general of the Army, an old soldier who was noncontroversial, largely because he had gone out of his way to make no enemies throughout his long and undistinguished career. He had never engaged in politics, so the radicals had nothing against him. On the other hand, Thomas had a personal ax to grind. He hated Secretary Stanton, who, on several occasions, had failed to give him the major field command for which he had yearned.

At 2:30 P.M. on February 21, 1868, two messages from the President were received simultaneously by the Senate and House of Representatives. One contained notification that Secretary Stanton had been irrevocably dismissed from office. The other named General Thomas as acting Secretary of War.

The Congress promptly went wild, with all other business forgotten. Some radical Republicans were outraged because President Johnson had deliberately thumbed his nose at them. Others were overjoyed, believing he had finally played into their hands and given them grounds for impeachment.

Messages were sent from Capitol Hill to the War Department, urging Stanton not to vacate his office. His friends told him to stay unless "minions of Johnson" removed him by force.

Never noted for his personal courage, Edwin Stanton literally barricaded himself behind the doors of his private office. He trusted no one, including his personal aides, and was so suspicious of anyone who came to the door that he even refused to admit the courier from his wife who was bringing him his meals. As a result he ate nothing for the next twenty-four hours.

Congressman Thaddeus Stevens, who was old, ill, and

on the verge of retirement, was ecstatic. "Now we've got Johnson," he exulted. "We're going to hang him!"

The Senate closed the press and visitors' galleries and went into executive session. In the debate that followed behind closed doors, radical after radical put his opinions of Andrew Johnson on the record. The meeting lasted until early evening, when it was reported that a resolution had been passed stating that "under the Constitution and the laws of the land, the President has no power to remove the Secretary of War and to designate any other officer to take his place."

In the House one of Stevens' most loyal followers, Representative John Covode of Pennsylvania, offered a succinct resolution: "Resolved, That Andrew Johnson, President of the United States, be impeached of high crimes and misdemeanors."

So many radicals clamored for the floor, wanting to put their low opinions of the President on the record, that the House did not adjourn until almost midnight. Long before that time Stevens had fallen sound asleep at his desk, and had to be awakened so friends could take him home.

Early the following morning General Thomas was placed under arrest. Instead of insisting on an immediate trial, as the President had told him to do, the old gentleman became confused and put up bail, which meant his case would be delayed. He then went to the War Department, where the situation degenerated into a farce. Almost as timid as the man he had been appointed to replace, Thomas complained bitterly to Stanton. Both men began to realize they were only pawns in a grim battle to the death between the President and the Congress, so they compromised by drinking the better part of a bottle of whiskey together. That night Stanton remained in the Secretary's office, while Thomas went home.

On February 22 the Senate conducted no business and adjourned hastily, and most members hurried to the House of Representatives so they wouldn't miss the high drama about to be enacted there.

The Democrats made a valiant but vain effort to come to the President's defense, but they were badly outnumbered. With radical supporters filling the galleries to overflowing, Republican after Republican arose to denounce Andrew Johnson in a mounting crescendo of epithet and invective. Seldom, if ever, had any man in public life been so reviled and scourged.

The galleries loved the demonstration, but more than twenty-five moderate Republicans were so disgusted they walked out of the chamber, as did the Democrats. The radicals were undeterred, however, and because others wanted to add their voices of hatred to the chorus, the debate was postponed from the twenty-second, a Saturday, until the following Monday.

The leadership was eager to get on with the hanging, so it was agreed that the vote on the impeachment resolution would be taken at 5 P.M. The last speaker was Thaddeus Stevens, who was succinct, saying that impeachment was "intended as a remedy for malfeasance in office and to prevent the continuance thereof." The sovereign powers, he insisted, rested in the Congress, who had been placed around the President as watchmen to force him to obey the law and the Constitution. His arguments were constitutional gibberish, but his listeners did not seem aware of it.

The vote in favor of impeachment was 126 to 47.

Every Republican voted in favor of the resolution, and every Democrat voted against it.

President Johnson remained remarkably calm. That evening several members of the Cabinet dined at the White House, and found him in a relaxed mood. His appetite was good, and he displayed an unusual sense of humor, telling several jokes. In the family quarters upstairs, Senator and Martha Patterson were apprehensive, and Mary Stover burst into tears. But Eliza Johnson was even more tranquil than her husband. "The governor," she said, calling him by the name she always used, "has done what's right, so the Lord will shield him and provide for him. Have faith in Almighty God, children, and you'll sleep as soundly tonight as your father and I will sleep."

A special House committee solemnly went to the Senate the following day and reported the impeachment resolution. The gravity of the occasion was somewhat spoiled, however, when it was discovered that the House, in its haste, had failed to draw up any specific charges of impeachment.

Much to the embarrassment of the radical leadership, the resolution had to be referred back to the House, where a new committee promptly went to work. This group had its hands full. Inasmuch as the President had committed no actual high crimes or misdemeanors, inasmuch as he had in no way actually violated the Constitution, it was very difficult for them to bring charges that made sense.

They tried, however, and finally put together thirteen vaguely worded charges, one to the effect that he had violated the Constitution.

When the news was reported to the President, he lost

his temper for the only time throughout the whole sorry farce. "Impeach me for violating the Constitution!" he shouted. "Damn them! I have been struggling and working ever since I have been in this chair to uphold the Constitution they trample underfoot! I don't care what becomes of me, but I'll fight them until they rot! I shall not allow the Constitution of the United States to be destroyed by evil men who are trying to ruin this government and this nation!"

The President quickly recovered his poise. That same night, accompanied by his daughters, he attended a reception at the home of Chief Justice Salmon P. Chase of Ohio, who would preside at his trial. Chase, a former senator who had entertained presidential ambitions, was assumed by the radicals to be strongly sympathetic to their cause, but they were shaken by Andrew Johnson's unexpected appearance under the Chief Justice's roof. Apparently it did not occur to the President's foes that the oath of office the Chief Justice had taken required him to deal impartially and fairly. As they saw the situation, all who failed to stand with them were their enemies. Thereafter they were careful not to confide in him, and treated him with an aloofness that verged on contempt.

Chase refused to be swayed by their ostracism. Although he was a man of limited intellect who had not distinguished himself in the Senate and was not adding new laurels to his reputation on the Supreme Court, he never lost his dignity, and he never forgot his obligation to the nation. Of all those who participated in the trial of Andrew Johnson, he—perhaps alone—emerged with his reputation unblemished.

As for the President, his self-control was remarkable.

95

Flanked by his daughters, he strolled through the rooms in which the reception was being held. His smile was unwavering. He offered his hand to those who were trying to drive him from office and disgrace him, and spoke with natural courtesy to everyone. All but the most militant radicals were impressed by his conduct.

In the days that followed, he continued to uphold the dignity of his high office, and his integrity under stress was unwavering. Various aides suggested that he use the powers of the presidency to win certain senators to his cause. He still commanded vast patronage, and could either offer jobs in the government to his followers or withhold such posts, depending on whether a senator indicated he might be amenable to a deal.

Johnson flatly refused to play such political games. His own fate was unimportant, he believed. It was the Constitution itself that was on trial, and the future of the United States depended upon the outcome. Consequently the case would be tried strictly on its merits, and he insisted that his own record remain clean.

He was encouraged by the unexpected support given him by ordinary citizens throughout the country. The charges against him were so blatantly exaggerated that thousands of people were offended, even in the states where the radicals were strong. Unprecedented quantities of mail arrived at the White House, and the President was inundated with letters. The ratio in his favor ran at a rate of more than five to one.

Many of the newspapers that had supported the radicals throughout the long crisis now became less aggressive, and a number ran editorials in which they wondered in print whether the vindictive representatives and senators were going too far. These editors wrote that, although they could not agree with Johnson's judgment in the conduct of the nation's affairs, they could not believe that he was guilty of having committed high crimes and misdemeanors.

Attorney General Henry Stanbery was determined to act as the President's principal attorney, and resigned from the Cabinet. In that way he was able to devote his entire time to the case, yet could not be criticized for performing the task at the expense of the public. As associates a number of distinguished lawyers were also retained, among them former Supreme Court Justice Benjamin Curtis of Boston, William M. Evarts of New York, and the President's own attorney from Tennessee, T. A. R. Nelson.

Their fees would have bankrupted Andrew Johnson, and a group of private citizens in New York and elsewhere offered to raise the necessary money. The President didn't want to be beholden to anyone, and refused the offer. The attorneys themselves solved the problem by announcing they were working on Andrew Johnson's behalf without compensation.

The House of Representatives appointed a special committee of seven members to act as "managers," or prosecutors, of the case. To the surprise of no one, Thaddeus Stevens was the chairman, but his health was so frail that Ben Butler was deputized to act as his first assistant.

On March 4, this group formally reported its charges to the Senate.

Three days later the Senate's sergeant-at-arms appeared at the White House and served the President with a summons that requested him to appear for the trial. He was ordered to present himself before the Senate at 1 P.M. on March 13.

Andrew Johnson accepted the document, and informed the sergeant-at-arms that he would "attend to the matter."

This reply, which was widely publicized, did nothing to satisfy the curiosity of those who wondered whether Johnson intended to confront the Senate in person. Only he and his attorneys knew his plans, and they kept their own counsel.

The demand for seats in the visitors' and diplomatic galleries was overwhelming, and it was said that speculators were offering as much as a thousand dollars for a pair of tickets. A carnival atmosphere prevailed in Washington, in spite of the gravity of the trial, and scores of newsmen descended on the city to augment the capital's press corps.

The President issued no public statement, and Chief Justice Chase refused to be interviewed. The radicals in both the Senate and House were less reluctant, however, and freely predicted that Andrew Johnson would be convicted.

Every aspect of the trial was examined under a microscope. Was it appropriate, the radicals asked, for Senator Patterson of Tennessee, the President's son-in-law, to attend as one of his judges when it was taken for granted he would vote for acquittal? The Johnson supporters countered with a question of their own: Was it appropriate for radical Ben Wade to sit in judgment, when he would succeed to the presidency if the incumbent should be found guilty?

The radicals attempted to win the support of major

Cabinet members, first sending a delegation to Secretary of State Seward. If he would abandon Johnson, he was told, Ben Wade would keep him as the senior member of the Cabinet.

Seward's reply was emphatic. "I'll see them damned first," he said. "The impeachment of the President is also the impeachment of his Cabinet."

Confident of success, the radicals also approached the President indirectly and offered to call off the trial if he would replace his present Cabinet with men of their own choice. Johnson refused the deal, and found it hard to express himself civilly.

On March 13, promptly at 1 P.M., the President's lawyers appeared at the Senate on his behalf and asked for a grace period of forty days so they could prepare their replies to the charges. They were granted a period of ten days.

Meanwhile Stanton, the direct cause of the controversy, remained in his office. He slept on a cot, ate meals sent in to him by his wife, and accompanied by the sentries who guarded him day and night, took short walks up and down the corridor outside his office. He was the forgotten man of the trial, and his wife repeatedly urged him to come home, because, she said, he was making an absurd spectacle of himself. But he was a prisoner of a situation he had helped create, and could not leave without incurring the wrath of the radicals on whom his political future—if any—depended.

On the morning of March 23, it was rumored that the President intended to face his tormentors in person, and a large crowd began to congregate at the Capitol. Hundreds more appeared outside the White House.

The first to arrive at the Senate were the House

"managers," who would prosecute the President, and they were greeted with a mixture of applause and jeers. Thaddeus Stevens was so weak that two of his colleagues had to assist him as he walked up the steps of the Senate.

Many of the senators went unrecognized and were able to slip into the Capitol without calling attention to themselves.

The crowd fell silent when Chief Justice Chase appeared.

Every time a carriage drew up at the entrance, people craned their necks and stared. But Andrew Johnson was not interested in creating a spectacle, and he disappointed the throngs. He had decided that the dignity of the office he held made it impossible for him to appear before the Senate in person. The radicals were even more disappointed than were the crowds outside, but there was no way to compel him to appear. He was already on trial, and there was literally nothing more they could do to him.

Promptly at 1 P.M., Chief Justice Chase rapped his gavel on the table, and the trial of Andrew Johnson began.

Counsel for the President rejected all thirteen of the charges against him.

That night, through no accident, the annual reception for the Congress was held at the White House. No single incident in Andrew Johnson's career better illustrates his courage, much less the stubborn lack of tact that had been one of the factors leading to his impeachment in the first place. Official Washington would have understood and no one would have blamed him had he chosen to postpone the reception indefinitely. It was surprising that he had elected to go through with the affair, and astonishing that it should take place on the very day that his trial had opened.

Neither then nor later did he indicate in writing why he was giving this particular affair on this occasion, and if he explained his motives to people close to him, they refrained from passing on his reasons for it. So posterity can only guess that he might have been thumbing his nose at his enemies.

However, he may have held the reception for a very simple reason. It was traditional for the President to entertain members of the Congress soon after March 4, the date when the new Chief Executive took office, and Andrew Johnson believed in the principle of observing tradition. Inasmuch as he displayed subtlety in few of his dealings, it is possible that he had little else in mind.

The reception was one of the most remarkable in the long history of White House social events. Staff members expected that only Johnson's supporters would appear, but they failed to take human curiosity into account. Radical Republicans and Democrats alike wanted to see for themselves how the President would act when he confronted his foes, and virtually every member of both the Senate and the House showed up.

The President, with Martha Patterson beside him, greeted his guests individually, then made a tour of the public rooms so he could chat with various senators and congressmen. Even those who hated him had to admit they could find no flaw in his conduct. He was courteous and charming to all, the perfect host, and made no mention of the trial that was unique in the history of the country. Some of his guests, unable to cope with his good manners, departed rather abruptly, while others remained until the affair ended. No harsh exchanges of words or other incivilities marred the occasion, and anyone who had expected verbal fireworks was disappointed. The President had proved he was a gentleman.

The next day the House "managers" began to call witnesses in an attempt to prove their charges. They failed from the outset, particularly when they summoned so-called character witnesses who were prepared to testify that the President habitually drank to excess. Johnson's counsel, on cross-examination, quickly established that these witnesses had never actually seen the President touch alcohol, but merely that they had "heard" he imbibed freely. Such evidence was admissible in no court.

The defense tried to establish from the outset that President Johnson had been eager to test the Tenure of Office Act in the Federal courts long before he had taken overt action by dismissing Secretary Stanton, but such witnesses as Secretary of the Navy Welles were not permitted to give testimony to that effect. Again and again, after Chief Justice Chase had ruled that such testimony was admissible, he was contradicted by the vote of the Senate. Although a two-thirds vote was necessary for conviction, procedural matters were settled by a simple majority vote, and witness after witness was gagged.

Ultimately General William Tecumseh Sherman was called to the stand. That hard-bitten warrior had no intention of being prohibited from telling the truth. For the better part of two days the radicals managed to stifle him, but the general was stubborn and unyielding, and before he left the stand he managed to place on the trial record a clear statement that the President had been eager from the beginning to test the validity of the Tenure of Office Act.

By the middle of April the strain began to tell on Andrew Johnson. Ben Butler and others vilified him in one vicious speech after another, but his defenders, including his own counsel, never replied in kind. The Tennessee stump speaker who always gave as good as he received in rough-and-tumble debate was outraged. He wanted to tear into his enemies in a public statement, and refused to listen when his lawyers told him he would do himself and his cause far more harm than good. When Martha Patterson explained the situation to her mother, however, Eliza Johnson intervened. She had a private talk with her husband, and the President promptly desisted. Her influence over him was still paramount, and her common-sense approach prevailed.

It was fortunate that Mrs. Johnson was able to restrain him. Various forces were at work on his behalf, and had he answered his enemies in kind, he might have negated them.

The charges against him could not be substantiated, and his foes were so unjust, so vituperative that a number of Republican senators found the actions of their radical colleagues difficult to digest. Prominent in this small group was Senator William P. Fessenden of Maine, a quiet, austere man who placed the demands of his own conscience above political considerations. He had never been friendly with Andrew Johnson. Their personalities had clashed, and they had long avoided each other.

In spite of their differences, however, Fessenden became convinced that the Republicans were failing in their efforts to prove that the President was guilty of high crimes and misdemeanors. He made no secret of his views, and as a consequence he was subjected to strong pressures from other Republicans to stand with them. When these efforts failed to move him, he received barrages of letters from his constituents in Maine, urging him to vote with the majority.

Fessenden held his ground, replying that he, not his constituents, had the obligation to vote. He realized that the people of Maine leaned heavily toward the radical position and that he would find it difficult to be reelected if he followed an independent course, but that did not deter him. The cause of justice, he told Senators Wade and Sherman, took precedence over his own career.

General Grant was not helping the President. The Republican convention would be held the following month, and he was the leading candidate for the presidential nomination. With the Democrats in disarray, he was certain to be elected if nominated, and he badly wanted to become President. Eager not to offend the radical majority for fear they might turn away from him, he lobbied quietly for Andrew Johnson's conviction. Grant was astute enough to take no public position and issue no statements, but in private he used his influence in attempts to persuade wavering senators to hold firm for conviction.

The President knew that the head of the army had joined forces with his foes, but refrained from rebuking him. Even in private he confined himself to the mild observation that he believed General Robert E. Lee, the Confederate commander, had been superior to Grant both as a strategist and as a tactician, a view that history has emphatically confirmed.

The behavior of Chief Justice Chase was far too impartial to suit the biased radical majority, and they saw to it that he suffered. He stopped receiving social invitations, and various senators made it plain to him that they would never support him for the presidency. He was badly upset by this attitude on the part of men he had regarded as friends, but he did not change his position.

In fact, he said in a letter to an old friend:

> How can the President fulfill his oath to preserve, protect and defend the Constitution, if he has no right to defend it against an act of Congress sincerely believed by him to have been passed in violation of it? To me, therefore, it seems perfectly clear that the President has a perfect right, and indeed was under the highest obligation, to remove Mr. Stanton, if he made the removal not in wanton disregard of constitutional law, but with a sincere belief that the Tenure of Office Act was unconstitutional, and for the purpose of bringing the question before the Supreme Court.

As the trial progressed, the Washington atmosphere became increasingly frenzied. Scores of professional gamblers had come to town, and were taking bets for and against conviction, with the odds swinging wildly from day to day. The rumor spread that the President intended to resign, that he had offered a compromise to the radicals, that he had lost his courage and intended to cave in. None of these possibilities materialized, and the President continued to live quietly, avoiding the limelight.

Senator Sherman of Ohio, possibly influenced by his brother's pro-Johnson position, tried to separate himself from the radical majority. But his colleagues exerted tremendous pressure to haul him back into line, and it appeared they would succeed.

Members of the diplomatic corps expressed admiration for the President, and their opinion was echoed by the press of Great Britain, France, Sweden, and the Netherlands. American newspapers that believed they had gone too far in supporting the radicals began to quote foreign editorials, thus backing off without openly losing face.

The Cabinet continued to give the President its firm, unwavering support. Both in public and in private most members agreed with Secretary of State Seward that the President would be exonerated, even though the Republicans commanded a vote sufficient to obtain the two-thirds majority necessary for conviction.

After his brief flareup in mid-April, Andrew Johnson grew calm again. He conferred for an hour or two each morning with his attorneys, but rarely mentioned the trial to anyone else. He avoided the subject at Cabinet meetings and presented a serene facade to visitors. Even when dining in private with his own family, he seldom referred to the matter.

He made only passing references to the trial in his correspondence, too, so it is impossible to judge his true feelings and state of mind during this period. His courage was undiminished, certainly, and his self-control did not falter. Secretary Welles said his appetite remained hearty, and every afternoon he continued to accompany his grandchildren on an outing to the banks of the Potomac River.

As nearly as can be determined almost a century later, Johnson's calm was genuine. He was fighting for the right as he conceived it, and he refused to descend to the level of his enemies.

The case dragged on into May, and attorneys of stature agreed that the radicals had failed to prove their charges against the President. Their success or failure was irrelevant, however. All that mattered was whether Andrew Johnson's foes could muster enough votes to convict him.

Early in May several Cabinet members privately drew up their own list of senators, and Secretary Welles wrote in his diary that he was afraid the President would be convicted.

On the same day, by coincidence, Senator Sumner made a list, too, and wrote he was afraid the President would be exonerated.

The vote was scheduled to be taken on May 12, and on that morning the United States Government was paralyzed. No one, the New York *Herald* reported, was at his desk; officials from the highest-ranking executive to the lowest clerk milled in the streets. No two head counts were identical, and everyone was guessing.

The law, Chief Justice Chase observed privately, had been virtually forgotten. Most senators were either against Andrew Johnson or for him, and the testimony that had been given during the trial was ignored.

The hour of decision was at hand for Andrew Johnson and the Republic.

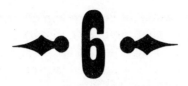

The radical Republican leaders in the Senate took a head count of their own shortly before they were due to assemble on May 12, and when they convened formally, they rammed through a postponement of the trial for four days. One of their number was ill, and they were afraid that without his vote they would fail to convict.

Tensions continued to build, and almost no work was done in government offices. The same atmosphere prevailed at the White House, but the President's private office proved to be an oasis of serenity. Andrew Johnson continued to greet visitors with courteous calm, and discussed many subjects without mentioning the trial. When speaking with old friends or members of the Cabinet, however, he displayed a tendency to reminisce about his boyhood, which was a new trait. When Martha Patterson and her husband confessed they were nervous about the outcome of the trial, the President teased them at the dinner table until they laughed.

During this final week of his ordeal, Andrew Johnson finally broke his self-imposed silence and granted several press interviews in which he summarized his position. He stressed his faith in the Constitution, said it was sheer nonsense that he wanted to create a revolution, and told a reporter from the New York *World*, which had consistently supported him, "When great questions are before the people, it is more important that they be understood than that anybody's dignity should be preserved. . . . Is it dignified of Mr. Wade to go around the country calling me a damned traitor? And must I be impeached if I say a word in reply?"

In the final days before the Senate vote was taken, it became apparent to the entire nation that nine Republicans favored acquittal. Such veterans as Fessenden, Grimes of Iowa, and Henderson of Missouri were hardened politicians whose careers were drawing to a close, and it was regarded as unlikely that they could be influenced by their radical colleagues.

A head count taken on May 15 convinced the Republican leadership they were one vote shy of conviction. Consequently they concentrated their attention on the youngest of their colleagues, forty-one-year-old Edmund G. Ross of Kansas, a newcomer to the Senate.

Of all members, Ross seemed the most likely to succumb to pressure. His experience was limited, and he had no political organization of his own back home on which he could rely for continuing support. In fact, Kansas was one of the most violently pro-radical, anti-Southern states, and Ross realized he would be signing his own political death warrant when he came up for reelection if he voted in favor of acquittal.

On the evening of May 15, several radicals dined with Ross, and they used every argument they could command in an attempt to sway him. At one point in the conversation he said—or seemed to hint—that the one charge on which the President might be guilty was Article XI of the indictment, an ambiguously worded paragraph dealing with the ouster of Stanton.

This slender thread of hope caused the Republicans to

alter their strategy for the following day. Instead of voting on each of the thirteen articles of impeachment in order, they would insist that the first vote be taken on Article XI. This strange procedure made no sense, but that didn't matter. They could place Article XI first on the agenda by a simple majority vote, and they didn't care what their opponents thought.

Meanwhile, the other Republican senators who were believed to favor acquittal were being subjected to strong pressures, too. John Henderson of Missouri received telegrams from St. Louis businessmen who had supported him financially in his election campaigns and who promised they would continue to support him if he voted "in the right way." The eleven members of the Illinois delegation in the House of Representatives held a meeting with Senator Lyman Trumbull. Their original intention was to present him with a solidly united front in favor of the President's conviction. But these men knew Trumbull had a rocklike integrity that could not be shaken, and five of the eleven came to him privately, one by one, prior to the meeting, and urged him to hold fast.

Senator Waitman Willey of West Virginia was a devout Methodist. It was no accident that he received a number of telegrams from high-ranking Methodist clergymen suggesting they would look with favor on a vote for conviction.

Promptly at noon on May 16 the Chief Justice called the Senate to order. The first order of business was that of placing Article XI at the top of the agenda, and this was done with dispatch, even though its legality was questionable.

Chief Justice Chase proceeded to admonish the crowded galleries. He would tolerate no interruptions, no demonstrations, no noise. If just one person, regardless of his status, uttered a sound, the galleries would be cleared. He then instructed the senators that no speeches or comments would be permitted. The clerk would call the roll, the Chief Justice would ask each in turn whether he found the President guilty or not guilty, and each senator would respond accordingly.

Chief Justice Chase's lecture to the spectators appeared to have been unnecessary, because an eerie quiet settled over the galleries. Everyone in the chamber was keeping a tally sheet of his own, or so it seemed.

Many of the senators looked haggard, and it was obvious that all of them realized they were making history.

They all took it for granted that the twelve Democrats would vote in favor of acquittal. Of the forty-two Republicans, a solid phalanx of thirty-three stood in favor of conviction. The hopes of both sides rested on the nine waverers.

Two of the nine switched at the last moment, and voted "Guilty." The other seven, among them Ross of Kansas, felt they were responsible only to their own consciences, and voted "Not Guilty." Thus the final vote was thirty-five to nineteen, one vote shy of conviction. The President was exonerated on the charge contained in Article XI.

Secretaries McCulloch and Welles awaited the results with the President in his office, along with General Thomas. A team of orderlies was on duty at nearby Willard's Hotel, which was connected to the Capitol by telegraph, to bring the returns to the White House as they came in.

President Johnson was the only member of the group

who displayed no tension. Welles later observed in his diary that he seemed to have no nerves.

The others, all armed with tally sheets, were grim, and their conversations were forced and stilted. But as the votes came in one by one, the President remained amiable, chatting about inconsequentials and telling little stories.

When it became evident that his enemies in the Senate could not convict him, he accepted the congratulations of his subordinates with a slight smile, then excused himself for a moment while he went upstairs to tell his wife the news.

Eliza Johnson accepted the verdict with a surface calm that matched her husband's. "I prayed," Martha Patterson later quoted her mother as saying, "and the Lord answered me."

Only when her husband bent down to kiss her did she give in for a moment, and her eyes filled with tears. Then she quickly flicked them away and urged her husband to return to his office.

By the time he went downstairs, other Cabinet members and various friends were arriving to offer him their congratulations. The President remained calm, displaying almost no emotion.

The joy of his followers was short-lived. The radicals, knowing they would be in trouble trying to obtain convictions on the remaining twelve articles of impeachment, voted by a simple majority to postpone the other votes for ten days. The President's ordeal now could not come to an end before May 26, at the earliest.

"Our hopes that we were out of the woods at last were dashed," Secretary Welles wrote in his diary.

Only the President himself refused to be disappointed by the delay. He knew the radicals would use every means at their disposal to persuade one or more of the Republican "renegades" to change votes, but his political sixth sense told him he was already in the clear.

For ten days the entire country lived in a state of almost unbearable suspense. For all practical purposes the Government stopped functioning, business dwindled at banks, and retail stores had so few customers that many closed their doors until the fate of the President was decided. Theaters were empty, as were restaurants, and in thousands of cities and towns only schools functioned normally.

The public at large rapidly developed an increasing sympathy for President Johnson. His exoneration on one charge convinced many that he was innocent on all charges, and the mail received at the White House doubled, then doubled again. Many newspapers, including scores that had demanded him impeachment, were now requesting that his ordeal be ended and that the Government resume its normal operations.

The President made no attempt to rally support, and reminded his Cabinet that he wanted no one to make any attempt to influence senators in his favor. "I see a victory ahead for the Constitution," he told Secretary Seward, "and I want nothing to spoil our chances."

The radicals felt no such constraint, and organized for a final effort to obtain the conviction of Andrew Johnson by any means at their command. A campaign was organized overnight to bring pressure on Lyman Trumbull, for example, and he received hundreds of telegrams, followed by thousands of letters, urging him to change his stand. If he failed to follow through accordingly, he was warned, his life would be in danger if he ever returned to Illinois.

Methodist Bishop Matthew Simpson again entered the fray. More of a politician than a clergyman, and a devoted radical at that, he exerted the full influence of his church in an effort to persuade the "backsliders" to change their position.

The radicals concentrated principally on Senator Ross of Kansas. He was offered a bribe and was told in so many words that he would be given literally any sum of money he wanted if he would change his position. When he made it clear that he had no interest in accepting a bribe, other means had to be devised.

Various radical leaders held long conversations with him, trying to persuade him to shift his vote. These efforts also failed, and in desperation the President's enemies sought the assistance of a young woman, a sculptress names Vinnie Ream. Ross, a bachelor, lodged at a boardinghouse kept by the girl's mother, and was believed to be interested in Vinnie.

So the radicals sent a delegation to call on her, and asked for her support. Her smile indicated to them that she was agreeable to the suggestion. What the radicals didn't know, however, and what she refrained from telling them, was that she was an ardent supporter of President Johnson. In the final days before the Senate reconvened, she gave Ross help of a far different kind, urging him to continue to vote according to the dictates of his own conscience.

It happened that the Republicans opened their national convention in Chicago during this interim period, meeting there on May 20. There was no question in the minds of the delegates that General Grant would win the nomination for President. He had no political affiliation, and the Republicans realized that if they failed to nominate him the Democrats would be sure to do so.

On May 21 Grant won the nomination by acclamation, with all 650 delegates voting for him.

Ben Butler and several other radicals conferred with Grant in private, and then went to Senator Henderson of Missouri. General Grant, they said, was certain to be elected. Henderson agreed. They then told Henderson that he would be appointed Secretary of War in the next Cabinet if he would change his impeachment vote.

Senator Henderson's frosty smile indicated that he couldn't be bribed, either.

On the morning of May 26, the Republican senators held a private caucus, and John Sherman of Ohio dismayed his colleagues when he told them he could not vote in favor of impeachment on Article I, which charged President Johnson with a direct violation of the Tenure of Office Act. Sherman said he had made it clear in speeches on the Senate floor that he believed Secretary Stanton had been exempted from the provisions of that act. Therefore, he would be inconsistent if he voted for impeachment on such grounds now.

Questioning by his colleagues revealed that he was still willing to vote for conviction on the remaining articles, however, so a new strategy was adopted. Article I would be dropped, and voting would begin with Article II.

A regular Cabinet meeting was being held that day, so all of the President's official family gathered at the White House. The members were aware of various efforts that had been made to persuade the seven reluctant Republicans to change their votes, and Secretary

Welles spoke for most of his colleagues when he said he was apprehensive. Only Secretary Seward and the President himself remained cheerful.

The same system that had been used ten days earlier was made operable again, with runners bringing the news to the White House from Willard's Hotel, where the votes were received by telegraph from the Capitol.

The Senate convened at noon, and the vote of a simple majority determined that Article II of the impeachment charges would be the first considered, with the others following in order. Because of Senator Sherman's stand, Article I was conveniently forgotten.

The Chief Justice issued another admonition to the galleries, and with the Senate again sitting as a High Court, the impeachment trial of Andrew Johnson was renewed.

One by one the senators voted. Fessenden of Maine did not change from "Not Guilty" to "Guilty." Neither did Fowler of Tennessee, Grimes of Iowa, or Henderson of Missouri.

At last it was the turn of Senator Ross of Kansas, and no one in the chamber spoke or moved as he rose to his feet. "I looked down literally into my open grave," he later said. A vote of "Not Guilty," he knew, could mean the end of a promising political career and would force him to change his whole way of life, which would include finding some new way to earn a living.

Displaying extraordinary courage, Ross voted, "Not Guilty."

When their turns came, so did Trumbull of Illinois and Van Winkle of West Virginia. Not one senator had changed, and impeachment was averted by a single vote.

In actuality, the vote was not as close as it appeared. Several senators, among them Sprague of Rhode Island, Morgan of New York and Willey of West Virginia had indicated privately that, if it became necessary, they were willing to change and to find the President innocent of the charges against him.

A vote was taken on Article III, and the results were the same.

By now the radicals knew they had suffered a total defeat, and wanted to adjourn. But Chief Justice Chase showed his mettle; other articles remained, and action had to be taken on them.

Rather than prolong the debacle, the radicals agreed to acquittal on all charges.

The trial was at an end, and Andrew Johnson's triumph was complete.

Less than a half hour after the final vote was taken, a messenger from the War Department brought the President Edwin Stanton's written resignation as Secretary. Stanton immediately vacated the office that had been his self-imposed prison.

Newspaper reporters, friends, and well-wishers came to the White House in large numbers, and an impromptu reception was held there. Everyone who saw the President was struck by his calm. He did not gloat, and when the press bombarded him with requests for comments, he refused to say anything derogatory about the men who had tried to dismiss him from office in disgrace. His dignity, the New York *Tribune* was forced to concede, "was monumental." And the Chicago *Tribune* observed, "Never has Andrew Johnson's stature been more Presidential than on this day of his great victory."

Years later, when Senator John Sherman wrote his autobiography, he confessed that although he had voted for conviction, he had been "well satisfied" with the result. His attitude was not unique. Sumner of Massachusetts, a pre-war Abolitionist who had long been a leader of the radicals, also admitted he had been mistaken.

At the time of their defeat, however, most of the radicals were furious, unwilling to concede that they had erred or had invented charges out of whole cloth in order to get rid of a man whose policies and approach to the problems of Reconstruction were so different from their own views.

Most of them remained vindictive, and they made their attitude clear when President Johnson reappointed Stanbery as Attorney General. It was necessary to send the appointment to the Senate for confirmation, and that body, in its wisdom, rejected the man who had been Andrew Johnson's principal attorney during his trial.

President Johnson was as loyal to his subordinates as they were to him, and was ready to do battle on Stanbery's behalf. But the former Attorney General, although grateful, was tired of controversy, and preferred to retire to private life. So the President submitted the name of Evarts, another of his lawyers, and by this time the radicals had subsided sufficiently for him to be confirmed.

It was Evarts who solved the problem of appointing a new Secretary of War. The radicals loathed General Thomas, and he would have been rejected had his name gone to the Senate. Evarts suggested General John M. Schofield, whose military record was above reproach and who had many friends in the radical camp, even though his own stand on Reconstruction was moderate.

When Schofield was summoned to the White House and offered the appointment, he asked for time to consider, then went privately to General Grant and asked his advice. Grant, who seemed virtually assured of election to the presidency, wanted to wash his hands completely of the Johnson Administration and urged his subordinate to refuse. He made the mistake, however, of saying that the President was "not to be trusted."

Schofield, a man of independent intellect and integrity, regarded the assessment as a gross exaggeration and was offended by it, so he accepted. The President was surprised and so was Schofield when they managed to establish a close working relationship.

The Democratic convention was scheduled to convene on July 4 in New York, and the vindicated President, had he wished, could have been his party's choice as their candidate. He would have been gratified by the opportunity to run against Grant and beat him, and there was no longer any doubt that public opinion had shifted in his favor.

Such staunchly Republican newspapers as the Boston *Advertiser*, Chicago *Tribune*, and Hartford *Courant* had been praising him since his vindication, and moderates of both parties, as well as many thousands of independent voters, admired the high-principled stand he had taken. A positive nod would have won him the nomination.

But his family wanted no more of life in Washington. The house in Greeneville had been restored and redecorated at last, and Mrs. Johnson, still ailing, was homesick. Martha Patterson, who had worked so hard and successfully as her father's hostess, had to think about her own growing family.

Andrew Johnson badly wanted the electorate's stamp of approval as a final vindication, but he bowed to the wishes of his wife and daughter. They had suffered during his long and cruel ordeal, and he felt he had no right to request that they make additional sacrifices for his sake.

So he made a choice that, in effect, was an abandonment of any hope that he might win election in his own right. If the leaders of the Democratic party came to him en masse and insisted that he run, he told his family, he would accept the nomination. If they did not, he would go home to Greeneville.

A Congressional vacation recess assured Andrew Johnson of the most pleasant summer he had yet known in the White House. His enemies had done their utmost to destroy him and had failed, and now they were no longer in session at the other end of Pennsylvania Avenue, subjecting him to their petty harassments.

His daily outings with his grandchildren were carefree, and for the first time in months laughter was heard at the dinner table. The entire family was looking forward to a return to Tennessee. Only the President himself secretly yearned for political vindication more complete than that which he had already achieved, but he unselfishly kept his thoughts to himself. Ultimately he would have his way, but for the present he would place his wife and family first.

When the Democrats assembled in New York they adopted a platform based on Andrew Johnson's fight against the radical Republicans in the Congress. The issues were clearly drawn, and it would have been logical for the party to nominate the President as their standard-bearer.

But Tammany Hall was emerging as the primary force in New York, and only by intervening directly could the President have won his party's support. He refused to take any active steps, just as he had refused to play politics to ward off the impeachment trial. His standards were unchanged.

After waiting in vain for the President to express himself, the Democrats began to look elsewhere. Chief Justice Chase would have been a logical candidate, but he—unlike the President—was torn. One day he wanted the presidency, but the next he preferred to keep his place as the country's highest-ranking member of the judiciary. As uncertain of his desires as they were of the President's, the Democrats turned to a relative nonentity, Horatio Seymour, who had been wartime governor of New York, and thereby virtually handed the Presidency to General Grant.

On August 11 Thaddeus Stevens died at his Washington boardinghouse. His funeral was held two days later, and President Johnson expressed a willingness to attend, hoping the gesture would prove he bore no animosity toward the old man who had been his principal enemy. Secretaries Seward and Welles dissuaded him, however, emphasizing that his presence would merely rekindle hard feelings. So the President remained at the White House.

The 1868 presidential campaign was one of the strangest ever waged, with the whole country acting as though the results were a foregone conclusion. General and Mrs. Grant retired to their modest farm in Illinois, and there they stayed, with the Republican candidate emerging only long enough to make a few token public appearances. Governor Seymour stayed in New York until early October, and when he finally went out on the campaign trail, he confined himself to a handful of desultory speeches.

Andrew Johnson, on whose record the campaign ostensibly was being fought, was not asked to participate, and he did not volunteer his services. For the moment, at least, he was tired of the political wars, and was content to stand aside. He was already making his own long-range plans, but told them only to his son-in-law, Senator Patterson.

So the campaign developed into a popularity contest between Grant, the North's military hero, and the intellectual Seymour, who was known only in New York. Even Seymour's most ardent partisans were willing to concede that Grant would win.

President Johnson had come to despise General Grant, whom he regarded as a two-faced betrayer. But he refused to castigate the Republican candidate in public, telling only his family and a few close friends what he really thought. "The country is making a mistake," he told Secretary Welles, "but in a democracy that is how people learn."

The initial phase of Reconstruction was drawing to a close. As the legislatures of the Southern states accepted the Fourteenth Amendment to the Constitution, which gave the vote to former slaves, they were being readmitted to the Union as full-scale partners, and President Johnson felt that, for the immediate present, his work was done. In midsummer he had issued an amnesty proclamation in which he granted pardons and restored the rights of citizenship to all who had participated in the war on the side of the Confederacy, excepting only Jefferson Davis and a few others who were under indictment. He had wanted to include them in the amnesty, but the members of his Cabinet persuaded him that the country was not yet ready for such a step. He indicated his willingness to wait until after the election to pardon the former President of the Confederate States, but left no doubt in the minds of his subordinates that he was planning such a move.

His attitude again illustrates the magnanimity of his spirit. President Johnson not only disliked Davis personally, but privately continued to regard him as a traitor. All the same, he believed the time had come for the entire nation to put the Civil War into the past, and he realized that Davis and the principles for which he had stood would not be forgotten until the man was pardoned. Consequently he was willing to lay aside his personal prejudices for the good of the nation as a whole.

General Grant, as anticipated, won the election by a landslide, and President Johnson sent the President-elect a courteous letter of congratulations, to which he received no reply. Then on Christmas Day Johnson granted an unconditional pardon to Jefferson Davis and the others who were also under indictment. For all he cared, he said, the radicals could rave, rant, and foam at the mouth. He was doing what he believed right and just, and there was no way they could stop him.

Early in December Robert Johnson had begun to pack his father's belongings, particularly his papers and other documents. The President issued orders to the White House staff that neither he nor any member of his family intended to take anything away except personal property.

On December 29, 1868, the Johnsons broke precedent by giving a children's ball for the sons and daughters of government officials, diplomats, and White House servants. No adults were invited, and the President's grandchildren acted as hosts and hostess. The party was a huge success, and Eliza Johnson made one of her rare public appearances. For a few hours hordes of youngsters demolished cakes, pies, tarts, and cookies, and bedlam reigned at the White House.

On New Year's Day the President gave the last of his major receptions, and government officials, diplomats, and members of both the Senate and House were invited.

General and Mrs. Grant deliberately absented themselves from the city so they would not not be obliged to appear, and a number of the senators who had voted in favor of impeachment also had the good sense to remain at home. There was something of a stir, at the height of the reception, when Congressman Ben Butler unexpectedly made his appearance. Even the President was momentarily nonplussed at the sight of the man who had called him an archtraitor in scores of speeches, but he recovered quickly and offered his hand to his foe.

In his final State of the Union message to the Congress, however, the President refused to compromise. Virginia, Texas, and Mississippi had not been allowed to participate in the presidential election because they had not yet ratified the Fourteenth Amendment, and the President declared in strong language that they had been denied their rights under the Constitution.

Certainly he had posterity in mind when he wrote:

"It may safely be assumed as an axiom in the government of states that the greatest wrongs inflicted on a people are caused by unjust and arbitrary legislation, or by the unrelenting decrees of despotic rulers, and that timely revocation of injurious and oppressive measures is the greatest good that can be conferrred upon a nation. The legislator or ruler who has the wisdom and the magnanimity to retrace his step when convinced of error will sooner or later be rewarded with the respect and gratitude of an intelligent and patriotic people.

There was little the radicals could do in the closing days of the Johnson Administration to insult the outgoing President, but they tried. The House of Representatives repealed the Tenure of Office Act, making it clear to Andrew Johnson that it had been intended exclusively as a means of placing a leash on him. He refused to reply to the slur.

In mid-February Robert Johnson and Mary Stover left Washington for Tennessee, taking all of the Stover and Patterson children with them, and went directly to Greeneville to prepare their parents' house for immediate occupancy.

On March 1, Eliza Johnson moved out of the White House, accepting an invitation from friends to be their house guest until her husband could join her.

Later that same day a new crisis erupted when General Grant informed the committee in charge of his inauguration that he would break precedent by refusing to ride in the same carriage with his predecessor. Badly upset, the members of the committee decided that they would have to provide two carriages, one for Grant and one for Johnson.

When Johnson was informed of the arrangements, he

merely smiled. Members of his Cabinet were indignant, but he urged them to calm themselves.

Martha Patterson was determined to turn over a spotless home to the new White House tenants, and not until late on the morning of March 4 did she or her husband depart.

Promptly at 11 A.M. a member of the outgoing White House staff released President Johnson's farewell message to the press. Its most significant passage read:

> My thoughts have been those of peace, and my effort has ever been to allay contention among my countrymen. Forgetting the past, let us return to the first principles of the government, and, unfurling the banner of our country, inscribe upon it in ineffaceable characters, *"the Constitution and the Union, one and inseparable."*

Neither Andrew Jackson nor Abraham Lincoln, who had so often stressed the same theme, could have expressed the conviction with greater clarity.

Soon after eleven, members of the outgoing Cabinet began to arrive, several of them disgruntled because they thought they would be forced to ride in Grant's inaugural procession. They found the President seated at his desk, methodically working his way through a mound of papers he was signing.

Attorney General Evarts was afraid they would miss the procession and did not even remove his greatcoat. The last to arrive was a cheerful Secretary Seward, who was smoking a cigar.

President Johnson continued to sign documents.

At eleven thirty-five, Seward suggested the group

leave at once so they wouldn't be late and hold up the inauguration.

"I think," Andrew Johnson said calmly, "that we will finish up our work here by ourselves."

He continued to sign papers until twelve o'clock, when his term of office came to an end.

Then he rose from his desk and, shaking hands with his Cabinet, thanked each member in turn for his loyalty and support.

Evarts held his greatcoat as he donned it, and Welles handed him his hat.

The entire White House staff awaited him on the portico, and some of the servants wept when he appeared.

"God bless you all," Andrew Johnson said, and descending the steps to his carriage, the seventeenth President of the United States drove off alone.

7

When Andrew Johnson left the presidency and joined his wife at the home of friends, he became a private citizen for the first time in thirty years. Contrary to the expectations of his family, he relished the experience, and for a week he lived a carefree existence, taking long walks, sleeping late in the morning, and dawdling over dinner.

Several newspapers had reported he was planning to make a trip to Europe, where his stand against the radicals was greatly admired. As a result a number of English, French, and German companies had offered him and his entire family free steamship accommodations, free meals, and free hotel rooms. After a lifetime of refusing to take favors from anyone, however, he could not bring himself to accept.

The city of Baltimore wanted to honor him before he returned to Tennessee, and he went there on March 12, expecting a modest celebration. The size and fervor of the demonstration touched him deeply. He spent the better part of the afternoon standing in the rotunda at the post office while literally thousands of men, women, and children filed past him, eager to shake his hand. That night hundreds of local and state officials and civic leaders attended a banquet and cheered him for hours.

On March 13, he returned to Washington, and for the

next few evenings attended dinners given for him by the members of his Cabinet. Eliza Johnson accompanied her husband on the night of March 17 when Welles was their host. Later the former Secretary of the Navy wrote in his diary, "No better persons have occupied the Executive Mansion, and I part from them, socially and politically, with regret."

The following morning Senator and Mrs. Patterson joined the Johnsons, and at noon all four boarded a private car on a train that would carry them to Tennessee. Members of the Johnson Cabinet and a few other friends saw them off, and in accordance with the former President's wishes there were no farewell ceremonies. No newspaper reporters were present either, the men bared their heads, and several of the ladies wept as the train pulled out.

It proved impossible for Andrew Johnson to keep his arrival in Tennessee private. Two railroad cars filled with friends from Greeneville and other towns in the eastern portion of the state joined him at Bristol, on the border, and at Greeneville itself he was greeted by brass bands, a parade in his honor, and fireworks.

He replied to the addresses of welcome, and later said it was the first time in years that he had enjoyed making a speech.

No sooner had the Johnsons settled into their refurbished house than the former President was inundated with speaking requests from all parts of the state. Union men had not forgotten his services to Tennessee and the country. Former Confederates, who had regarded him as an archenemy, now recognized him as their champion. Former slaves lauded him for his fairness and his genuine desire to help them improve their lot. To the small farmers, artisans, and "mechanics," he was the great man he had always been.

The invitations he received were so pressing, so insistent that after spending less than a week at home he went off on a junket that took him to Knoxville, Chattanooga, and Memphis, as well as a number of smaller communities. Everywhere he was greeted with an enthusiasm unmatched since the time of Andrew Jackson.

The last stop was Nashville. The capital turned out en masse, and thousands filled the streets when he delivered an impromptu address from a second-floor balcony in the St. Cloud Hotel. He struck themes familiar to anyone who had followed his career, but never had his spirit of rugged independence been more pronounced. He said, in part:

> When I was inaugurated President I felt that if the destruction of the government could be arrested until the whole American people could be aroused, that they would come to the rescue and save the Constitution and the country.
>
> I ask nothing at your hands. I feel prouder today, standing in your midst, privileged and authorized to advocate those great principles of free government, than I would of being President on the ruins of the Constitution of my country. I intend to appropriate the remainder of my life, short as it may be, in the vindication of my character and that of the state.
>
> It is my own choice to come to my own state and lay my weary bones down in peace. And, if I can do nothing more, I will adopt the language of Cato [the Younger]. When Caesar was making his inroads upon him, Cato said to his son, "Retire to the Sabine fields, and there with a pure and sincere heart, if you can do nothing more, pray

for Rome." If I can do nothing more, I can retire to my humble home, and with a good conscience I can pray for my country. I feel prouder in retirement than imperial Caesar, for, my countrymen, in these corrupt times when "vice prevails and impious men bear sway, the post of honor is a private station."

I accepted the Presidency as a high trust, not as a horn of plenty, with sugar plums to be handed out here and there to that individual who had presented the greatest gift.

I stand before you unscathed, and put the whole pack at defiance. Thank God I can stand before the people of my state and lift up both my hands, and say, in the language of Samuel, "Whose ox have I taken, or whose ass have I taken? . . . At whose hands have I ever received bribes, and had my eyes blinded?" If there is any, let them answer, and I will return it. Thus I return to you, feeling in my own conscience that I have discharged my duty as a faithful man.

He was cheered repeatedly, and the crowd called him back to the balcony again and again. The spontaneous demonstration ended when the people serenaded him. There were tears in his eyes as he watched the throng disperse.

In his own way Andrew Johnson had served emphatic notice on the radical Republicans that he had no intention of spending the rest of his life in passive retirement. For the immediate present, he needed the rest that his wife insisted he take, but ultimately he would return to the battle. The enemy had struck the first blow, but he intended to strike the last.

Certainly the new administration was providing him with ample ammunition. Grant was already demonstrating that as President he was an inept bumbler, with little control over his subordinates, who were accepting graft on an unprecedented scale. Ultimately the Grant administration would prove to be the most corrupt in the century-old history of the United States.

It was the former President's firm intention to remain on the sidelines and give the new administration time to hang itself before he became active again. But state and local elections were being held in Tennessee in August 1869, and when a delegation of Democrats came to Greeneville, Andrew Johnson could not resist their request for help. He stumped the state on their behalf, and the results were overwhelming. His candidate was elected governor by a majority of more than fifty thousand votes, the largest on record, and the Democrats easily won both houses of the legislature.

Newspapers throughout the country took note, and many observed that the former President was still a power in the land.

Gradually he established a new routine. He spent a great deal of time taking care of his wife, whose physical condition made it difficult for her to leave the house. Each day he spent an hour or two dictating reminiscences to a secretary, and every afternoon, no matter what the weather, he took a long, brisk walk. He knew most of his fellow townsmen by name, and was always willing to chat, provided the passerby fell in beside him and walked with him. Only on rare occasions was he willing to interrupt his stroll by stopping.

Democrats in and out of Tennessee repeatedly urged him to run for the United States Senate, but he was in no hurry. His long career had taught him patience, and he preferred to wait until, in his opinion, his return to

Washington would create the greatest impact on the people. His mail, which was heavy, told him that Americans everywhere were growing disillusioned by the corruption and ineptitude of the Grant administration. Moderate Republicans were beginning to vote the Democratic ticket in local and state elections,and radicals were becoming more moderate in their views. There was already talk of "the good old days" of former President Johnson's administration.

In 1871, some of Andrew Johnson's friends entered his name as a candidate for the Senate without bothering to find out his own wishes in the matter. He was not displeased, however, and decided to leave his name on the list, even though he did no campaigning, made no speeches, and issued no statements. In spite of his passive approach, he was almost elected, and he knew that when he really wanted the position, he would not find it difficult to attain his goal.

The Southern states had been restored to the Union in good standing, but the radicals continued to hobble them in politics. As a consequence, relations between whites and blacks deteriorated rapidly and were further complicated by the rise of the Ku Klux Klan, which used terror as its principal weapon.

Andrew Johnson had warned the country of the consequences of the radicals' Reconstruction policies, and all of his dire predictions were materializing. President Grant was unable to control a rampant Congress, and the nation, although continuing to expand industrially, was floundering.

In 1872, a group calling themselves Liberal Republicans broke away from their party and nominated editor

Horace Greeley for President; subsequently he was also endorsed by the Democrats. The regular Republicans, who had no real alternative, nominated Grant for a second term.

Andrew Johnson roused himself and began to campaign actively on behalf of the Democrats. A number of friends tried to persuade him to become a candidate for congressman-at-large, even though both the Democrats and Republicans had candidates in the field. His entry into the race, they argued, would give him a valid reason to stump the entire state.

He had no political organization of his own and wanted none, but ultimately he gave in to his friends' pleas, although he knew his chances of winning were slim. His campaign was arduous, and took him from one end of Tennessee to the other. In all, he made more than two hundred speeches. He wasted no time on a discussion of local issues, and talked only about his own policies as President. The radicals were still in control in Washington, he declared, and were ruining the country.

Somewhat to his own astonishment Andrew Johnson came within a hair of winning the election. This was a remarkable achievement in view of the fact that his was essentially a one-man campaign in an election that returned the opposite party to office. Newspapers throughout the state agreed that he was Tennessee's most beloved citizen, that he had strengthened his hold on the people and that, if he wished, he could be elected senator or governor.

The former President was satisfied with what he had accomplished, and returned to his quiet Greeneville life, which was punctuated by the visits of his grandchildren.

The New York *Post* and the Chicago *Tribune* wanted to send reporters to Tennessee to interview him, but he declined, saying the time was not yet ripe.

In 1873, a financial panic swept the United States, and millions lost their jobs. But even the coming of hard times did not prevent some of President Grant's key subordinates from accepting graft.

The country as a whole was fed up, and the elections of 1874 produced a Democratic majority in the House of Representatives, the first in fourteen years. The excesses of the Grant administration made the voters realize that their elected representatives were still crippling and humiliating the defeated South. Almost a decade had passed since the war had ended and the radicals' loss of seats in both the Senate and the House offered hope that the action could not be reunited.

Andrew Johnson knew the time had come to vindicate himself and his policies. At the age of sixty-six he was still vigorous, alert, and healthy, and it did not matter that his hair had turned gray, that his face was lined. The Tennessee legislature, its members responding to the will of the people, was scheduled to elect a new member of the United States Senate.

Only one ex-President had ever returned to the Congress, John Quincy Adams, who served in the House for many years after his term of office had ended. Now another former President decided to return to politics.

Andrew Johnson announced that he was a candidate for the Democratic nomination. He was the first to enter the contest, and he inaugurated his campaign without delay. Most Tennessee politicians agreed with out-of-state observers that it would be almost impossible for any opponent or combination of opponents to defeat him, but he was taking no unnecessary risks. He covered the entire state, speaking in cities and towns and in villages of only a few hundred inhabitants. He shook thousands of hands. Everywhere he held meetings in which he urged citizens to express their opinions of current national and international affairs. After six years of waiting, the former President was ready for action, and intended to let nothing stand in his path.

The radical Republicans were equally determined to block his return to Washington, and outside organizers poured into the state, their pockets bulging with money. They decided to employ divide-and-rule tactics, and the names of five other candidates were placed in contention, with the radicals hoping that no one could obtain a majority of the vote.

Andrew Johnson proved he had learned a great deal and forgotten little during a lifetime in politics. The balloting lasted a full week, and the former President, starting with a hard core of thirty-five supporters, patiently chipped away at his opponents, adding newcomers to his list by ones and twos. Suddenly the opposition caved in, and more than two thirds of the legislators flocked to his banner.

Now he was senator-elect, and the newspapers of Tennessee rejoiced. Republican as well as Democratic editors hailed his victory. Some even suggested that he consider running for a second term as President the following year.

Newspapers in other parts of the country expressed pleasure, too. The New York *Herald* said:

> Fortunately Mr. Johnson has lived to see his vindication. Because the American people know him so well,

because he was impeached and hounded as a traitor and chained and handcuffed by Congress, the contest in the Tennessee legislature possessed a national interest and is really a national victory. He is the best man Tennessee could have chosen, not merely for herself but for democracy of North and South. The Senate needs men who have the courage to speak the truth. . . . It is now generally conceded that the imaginary misdemeanors of 1868 were in fact official merits.

The New York *World* was delighted by "the return of so experienced and upright a man as Mr. Johnson to the Senate. His election. . . . is a public boon. Mr. Johnson's past proves that his future course will be unselfish, honest and very courageous."

The New York Times was equally laudatory: "We shall not be sorry to see him again in public life. Whatever his faults as President may have been, at any rate he went out of the White House as poor as he entered it and that is something to say in these times. The public generally takes a more favorable view of Mr. Johnson's character now."

The Democrats in the Senate were pleased by his election, although they realized it was unlikely he would respond to party disciplines but would vote as he wished. The Republicans were perturbed, and those who had voted in favor of his impeachment were openly unhappy. Certainly it had never occurred to them, when they had tried to hound him out of office, that he would become their colleague.

President Grant's thoughts are unknown, but it must have occurred to him that his predecessor would show him little mercy.

Letters of congratulations swamped the Greeneville post office, among them a warm note from Mrs. William T. Sherman.

One note, written in Lawrence, Kansas, was of particular interest:

> I am rejoiced to learn this evening of your election to the Senate. Your vindication from the slanders born of the hatred & malice of the impeachers in 1868 is now well nigh complete. I trust that the reign of hate has gone by & that a better day is coming.
>
> Excuse the unconventional form of this note. I write it in haste at my journeyman printer's desk as I am able to snatch a moment from my evening labors.

The signature was that of "E. G. Ross," the former Kansas senator, who was still paying a high price for having dared to vote according to his conscience in the impeachment trial.

President Grant called the Congress into special session early in March 1875, and Andrew Johnson made plans to go to Washington alone. His wife's physical condition made it impossible for her to accompany him, and his daughters were busy with the affairs of their own families.

Senator-elect Johnson arrived in Washingtion on the afternoon of March 5, and as he had told no one his precise plans, he was met by neither friends nor supporters. He went by carriage to Willard's Hotel on Pennsylvania Avenue, where the press awaited him, and he was interviewed in the sitting room of his suite.

The questioning began on a light note. One reporter gestured toward the White House, plainly visible through the windows, and commented that his present accommodations weren't as spacious as those to which he had last been accustomed.

"True," he said with a smile, "But they are more comfortable."

The key question was asked by a representative of the New York *Tribune*. "Will you not in your new position have an opportunity to pay off some old scores? You must have a mass of facts against many of the leaders of the parties of today."

The reply was succinct: "Whatever I may have I do not say, but I shall use nothing. I have no enemies to punish nor friends to reward."

That night the senator-elect dined quietly at his hotel with his Tennessee colleague and protégé, Senator Henry Cooper, and the following day, promptly at noon, a page conducted him to his seat in the Senate chamber. The galleries were jammed, even though a heavy snow had fallen that morning, and the spectators applauded him.

A number of his old enemies were still members of the Senate, and others had moved up from the House of Representatives. Among them were Sherman of Ohio, Anthony of Rhode Island, Freylinghuysen of New Jersey, Howe of Wisconsin, Cameron of Pennsylvania, Conkling of New York, and Morrill of Maine. Boutwell of Massachusetts and Logan of Illinois had been members of the House committee that had been in charge of the impeachment prosecution. Vice President Henry Wilson, who was presiding, had been a senator six years earlier and had voted for impeachment.

Senator Edmunds of Vermont, who had voted for impeachment, was speaking when Andrew Johnson walked into the Senate chamber. He looked over his shoulder, then became so flustered that he knocked a stack of books off his desk onto the floor. Other pro-impeachment senators either became very busy studying documents on their desks or stared straight ahead.

The swearing-in ceremonies took place without delay. Johnson was preceded by Hannibal Hamlin of Maine, who had been Vice President during Abraham Lincoln's first term, and he had not yet returned to his seat.

Senator Cooper escorted his colleague to the front of the chamber. Vice President Wilson, in a marked gesture of respect, came down from the dais to administer the oath of office.

The oath taken, Senator Johnson immediately made his feelings plain by offering his hand to the Vice President, then to Hamlin. The galleries applauded wildly.

As the new senator from Tennessee returned to his seat, a page brought him a huge bouquet of flowers, and for the first time he displayed emotion, and tears appeared in his eyes. Again the galleries erupted.

In order to keep other demonstrations from interrupting the business of the Senate, Johnson retired to a cloakroom. There he was soon surrounded by colleagues who came to offer their congratulations. The first of the pro-impeachment senators to appear was John Sherman of Ohio, and Andrew Johnson unhesitatingly and cordially shook hands with him. Subsequently he did the same with virtually all the others who had been his foes. He was demonstrating that he bore no personal grudges, and his integrity was so great that his former foes took him at his word.

Thereafter he was accepted without question as a member in good standing of what was already being called "the world's most exclusive club."

The Government was enmeshed in a nasty crisis that had aroused the entire country. The franchise was still being denied most whites in Louisiana, so the affairs of the state theoretically were being conducted by black members of the legislature. Most were illiterate, however, and were being used by carpetbagging interlopers from the North, who were stealing fortunes at the expense of all the people of the state.

Two opposing factions of carpetbaggers put up different candidates for the governorship of Louisiana. The stronger of them included President Grant's brother-in-law, and supported a man named Kellog. The situation was so confused that blacks and whites both rioted.

President Grant intervened, and declared that Kellog was the legitimate governor of Louisiana, a move of dubious legality. Then he ordered General Philip Sheridan to back up his selection with troops. Sheridan imposed martial law on the entire state, and his bayonets imposed order.

As if these developments were not bad enough, the undiplomatic Sheridan created yet another storm by making a public statement to the effect that the whites of Louisiana were "banditti," and that he intended to deal with them accordingly.

These blunders outraged the entire country. Southern whites and men of reason in the North believed the whites of Louisiana were being treated unfairly. Northern blacks were indignant because they realized the blacks of Louisiana were being manipulated like puppets. And men of goodwill everywhere were incensed because the President had suspended civil government and had sent in troops.

The situation was so delicate that the subject had not been raised in either the Senate or the House. The Republicans were embarrassed by Grant's bumbling, ashamed of the open graft taken by people who were close to him, and they wanted to sweep the whole Louisiana mess under a rug. The Democrats, although commanding a majority, were afraid that any speeches they might make would simply inflame the people of Louisiana, and they didn't want to be held responsible for further bloodshed.

Meanwhile, Andrew Johnson remained quiet and for two weeks took part in the routine business of the Senate. During that time he assessed the situation in Louisiana, learning all he could about it, and when the crisis showed no signs of easing, he decided the time had come for him to speak.

The problem, a direct outgrowth of the Reconstruction policies he had fought, was made to order for him. It was absurd that, a full ten years after the war had ended, the South was still being subjected to treatment as an occupied land. He made his preparations with greater care than usual, and on March 22 he rose from his seat in the Senate chamber and asked for the floor. Other senators could not speak on the subject, but Andrew Johnson was incapable of remaining silent.

It had been rumored that he would make a major address on the twenty-second, so the galleries were filled, and the presence of a large number of reporters indicated he would have press coverage throughout the country. This suited his purposes, as he was speaking to the American people, not merely to their elected representatives in the Senate. Here was his opportunity for vindication, the chance he had been awaiting ever since his old enemies had handcuffed him and tried to expel him from office.

His speech, delivered with all of the oratorical fervor at his experienced command, created a sensation throughout the United States. It made headlines everywhere, and most major newspapers published long excerpts. In the closing chapter of his long, painful war with his short-sighted enemies, Andrew Johnson was having the last word. He sought neither retribution nor vengeance, but his last address was one of his best, and was the fitting climax of a career that had extended over the better part of a half century.

Among his key passages were the following:

> Where are we going, Mr. President? Is Louisiana a commonwealth as it now stands? Or is her government maintained by military power, and that through the President of the United States? Is it his government? . . . It is not his place to interfere with either of the contending powers.
>
> Why was Kellog made governor? Was it for the purpose of irritation, for the purpose of getting up insurrection, so as to raise the cry, "These Southern people are in revolt"? The people of Louisiana were anxious for full restoration to the Union, but what is that to those acting behind the curtain and who are aspiring to retain power, and if it cannot be had by popular contest, would inaugurate a system of terrorism, and in the midst of the war cry triumphantly ride into the Presidency for a third Presidential term. And when this is done, farewell to the liberties of the country!

How far off is empire? How far off is military despotism?

Sheridan says the people are all banditti, and if he had a military commission the President need not disturb himself any further, for he would manage all the rest! . . .

Give me back the Constitution of my country unimpaired! Give me back the Constitution of my country! In the language of Webster, let this Union be preserved "now and forever, one and inseparable." Let us stand equals in the Union, all upon equality. Let peace and union be restored to the land. May God bless this people, and God save the Constitution.

The speech was applauded from coast to coast, and even newspapers that had continued to support the radical approach to Reconstruction declared that only Johnson's way would restore unity, peace, and prosperity to the country.

President Grant had been hinting broadly to friends and associates that he wanted a third term, but his predecessor's address restored perspectives. Whatever chance Grant may have had of being elected again faded overnight, and he was compelled to think in terms of retirement.

The special session of the Congress ended a few days after Andrew Johnson made his speech, and he returned to Tennessee in triumph. Everywhere in the United States, it seemed, men spontaneously and simultaneously conceived the same idea: return Johnson to the White House! Not only were powerful Democrats in every state intending to make him their candidate, but many in the increasing ranks of the moderate Republicans were eager to jump on his bandwagon. There seemed little doubt that, if he wanted the presidency again, it would be his.

The man who had escaped conviction by a single vote achieved a level of popularity he had never before known. The New York *World* called him "the greatest of living Americans," and scores of other newspapers agreed.

Another year would pass before the major parties held their nominating conventions, so there was no immediate need for Johnson to make up his mind about running. He went straight home to Greeneville, and told his wife and children that he had no desire for another term as President, but that he would be willing to serve if the country really needed him. He would see what developed in the next six to eight months before he made up his mind, and until then he would not commit himself one way or the other.

All through the spring and early summer he stayed at home, living quietly with his wife. He rejected all requests for newspaper interviews, and he turned down the many speaking engagements offered to him. Martha Patterson believed that having achieved the total vindication he had sought, he was satisfied and wanted nothing more in life.

Late in July, he went off to the Stover house to visit Mary and his grandchildren. Never had he been more serene. He indicated to his daughter that he hoped he would be able to retire permanently after serving the rest of his term in the Senate.

On the morning of July 29, 1875, Andrew Johnson awakened with a splitting headache. Before he could leave his bed he was stricken with a massive heart attack, which was diagnosed by the physicians of the period as apoplexy. He soon lapsed into a coma from which he never recovered.

Prominent physicians hurried to his bedside, but they were powerless to help him. The Pattersons brought Mrs. Johnson to the Stover farm so she could be near her husband when the end came. His illness was short, and at dawn on the morning of July 31 the heart of Andrew Johnson, seventeenth President of the United States, stopped beating.

In accordance with a request he had made two years earlier, he was buried on the top of a hill overlooking Greeneville. His body was wrapped in a flag of the United States, and a copy of the Constitution was his only pillow.

The funeral was simple, in keeping with the way he had lived, and thousands of ordinary citizens, people on whose behalf he had worked so long and hard, followed his coffin to its last resting place.

SELECT BIBLIOGRAPHY

Bacon, G. W., *Life of Andrew Johnson*, London, 1913.

Beale, Howard K., *The Critical Year: a Study of Andrew Johnson and Reconstruction*. New York, 1930.

Bowers, Claude G., *The Tragic Era: The Revolution After Lincoln*, Boston, 1929.

Burgess, John W., *Reconstruction and the Constitution*. New York, 1902.

Cowan, Frank, *Andrew Johnson, President of the United States: Reminiscences of His Private Life and Character*, Greensburg, Pa., 1894.

DeWitt, David M., *The Impeachment and Trial of Andrew Johnson*. New York, 1903.

Grant, Ulysses S., *Personal Memoirs*. New York, 1886.

Hamilton, J. C. de R., *Life of Andrew Johnson*. Greeneville, Tenn., 1928.

Johnson, Andrew, *Papers*, Library of Congress.

——, *Speeches*, ed. by Frank Moore. Boston, 1876.

Laski, Harold J., *The American Presidency: An Interpretation*. New York, 1940.

Lomask, Milton, *Andrew Johnson, President on Trial*. New York, 1960.

McKitrick, Eric L., *Andrew Johnson and Reconstruction*. Chicago, 1960.

Milton, George F., *The Age of Hate: Andrew Johnson and the Radicals*. New York, 1930.

Ross, Edmund G., *History of the Impeachment of Andrew Johnson*. Sante Fe, N.M., 1896.

Savage, John, *Life of Andrew Johnson*. New York, 1866.

Seward, Frederick W., *Andrew Johnson*. Philadelphia, 1890.

Stampp, Kenneth M., *The Era of Reconstruction*. New York, 1965.

Stryker, Lloyd Paul, *Andrew Johnson, a Study in Courage*. New York, 1929.

Thomas, Lately, *The First President Johnson*. New York, 1968.

Welles, Gideon, *Diary*, ed. by Howard K. Beale. New York, 1960.

Winston, Robert, *Andrew Johnson, Plebian and Patriot*. New York, 1928.

INDEX

151